The Awkward Armadillo

A Mental Health Memoir

Aimee Larson

Getting This Book Started: Aimee Style

I have written poems (no, nothing published) and have dabbled in short stories (also never published or shared for that matter). I have always had this idea of writing my memoir. I set up a date to finish it but would never meet that date, which was discouraging. I was belittling myself. We are our own worst enemy, of course. I would write and write... then stare at the screen, save the file and never look at it again. Why? Because the voices in my head told me certain things, most of them a lot like: "You'll never be good enough." Unfortunately, this happened in many other areas of my life as well.

I asked myself, "Why would you think someone would be interested in your life? Why would people want to read this?" Then I did something different. I started putting my energy into words. I attempted to make sense of everything around me. My goal was to connect with other people who might benefit from some portion, or perhaps all, of my story. I'm an awkward, odd person who grew up in a dysfunctional family. There are portions of this book that you may or may not relate to...but I hope you can at least enjoy my awkward random journey through it all.

The memories within these pages contain both the hilarious and the dark parts of my life. Life is full of experiences that continue to shape who we are as individuals. Each crack is loud or silently identifiable. It entirely depends on how we take things in, and how our environment responds to us, even though our surroundings don't include magical dragons and unicorns.

Side Note: Unicorns and dragons would be unique and would trump the need for a vehicle any day. There is this a beauty in the screams and monsters we fight each day. People that fight for their sanity every day, are the true warriors. This is why I took a deep breath and dove in, in hopes of even helping one person smile.

These pages contain my truth, albeit slightly altered to protect those that are in my life. I've changed my name to Aimee and changed the names of individuals in my story to protect their identities. Or perhaps I want to feel like a Batman and Iron Man combo, mysterious attitude coupled with 'this is who I am.'

What would you even call that superhero combo? "Iron Bat" or "Bat Iron?" Either way, you can call me as you like. Each story revolves around my mental health journey, which sadly does not involve real-life dragons or unicorns (spoiler alert). In our society, many people push away their demons and throw them into fictional characters. Or perhaps dismiss other people's demons. "You can't be depressed; you have everything to live for." The beast exists. Watching and poking at every little piece of life. Making life harder to adjust to and move through, having to bear the extra weight the demon carries. This is my story, wandering through the social bits of life.

Intermixed throughout the severe parts are bits of humor and randomness. You have been forewarned. Hopefully you are prepared to read with a "forward and upward" mindset the crazy life of somebody you don't know. Please do not give this to your young child in elementary school. I swear, I make up words in this book, and I mention the exquisite pleasures of women's puberty and madness. Thanks!

P.S. People can be difficult, beneficially, or in a bad way. Thus, if I accidentally offend, make you cry, etc. I apologize in advance. But, life is strange and also filled with comedy. Or life is strange and so it is a comedy. This book contains topics into anxiety, depression, abuse, mentions of alcohol and death.

"Be yourself; everyone else is already taken."

Oscar Wilde

Contents

CHAPTER 1
Childhood Anxiety, Bullies and IEP

When I was little, my mother and father would discuss my individual quirks and odd personality with my teachers. They would carry folders of my IEP (Individual Education plans) regarding my speech and learning disabilities, with sprinkles of reading comprehension issues and a dose of anxiety. My parents avoided using the term "anxiety." Instead, they went through my warning label, the same way you would read one on your sensitive, dry-clean-only jacket.

My warning label might read something like this: Do not leave unattended. Will get easily distracted by animals, Beanie Babies, rocks (will try to sneak rocks in pockets off school property). Do not communicate that you will call the parents. No matter what you say afterward, she will comprehend it as, "I am in trouble." Just contact us regardless, whether or not she is in trouble. We do not want her to have a panic attack or shut down in front of everyone. Also, she is an awkward kid. You have been warned of our sensitive daughter. Should we get you white or red wine?

My parents never really wanted to admit that I had an anxiety issue. They grew up in the '60s and '70s when mental health wasn't anything anyone wanted to discuss. Everything that happened in the family stayed in the family, along with packs of beer, cigarettes and hidden bruises. My parents each grew up with one abusive person in their family. My father's dad was also an alcoholic and abusive individual after fighting in World War II. My mom's mom was an alcoholic and a narcissist. No one ever talked about what was going on in the household. Those in Fight Club never spoke about Fight Club—the same thing occurred when dealing with issues at home. People rarely spoke up about what was going on at home. They separated their home life and school life.

Both my grandparents lived about a block away from each other, which is how my parents met. Perhaps that was one of the major reasons their love flourished— the identification and familiarity with growing up in a destructive household. As young adults, they entered each other's lives and found familiarity in the toxic life they each lived. The abuse, the heartache and wanting to push through the hardships. They ended up moving about two hours away and started a family of their own. A family they wanted to ensure did not go through the same abuse or hardships they themselves went through. Which, I suppose brings me back to their overprotective side when it came to my education.

My elementary school teachers would brush the warning label under the ground, as my parents were what they would call "worry warts" for their only daughter. The truth of the matter was, yes, my parents were "worry warts." They were not wrong, though, regarding how I perceived the world. I would smile and laugh and have tremendous difficulty verbalizing what I wanted to say. Any instance where I thought I would get in trouble, I would cry. Even for minor things—if a teacher corrected me on how I held my pencil, I cried and completely shut down. While I do not remember these individual events, I remember them as a collection of sensitive reactions to being corrected. I was that odd girl that no one wanted to talk to, because I would get so nervous and overstimulated with everything going on. Too much noise, too much talking in the background... everything felt too much to pay attention to.

Sure, sometimes I did not care or fear—but those days were few and far between. The ultimate horror was being called on the first day of class to introduce myself. Where do you begin in a classroom full of people? People that know how to communicate with one another.

"Let's play a game. Tell us three things about yourself. Two lies and a truth. We have to guess which one is true," the teacher would say.

In a faraway magical world, I might be a great communicator and speaker of different languages. I'd have no trouble saying, "Well, I can pull a bunny out of my pocket. Second, I can make up any language on the spot. Third, I overthink everything." Spoiler Alert: The ability to overthink everything is the truth. The other two are lies. Even in this far-off magical world,

I'm sure a group similar to PETA would be all over me for pulling bunnies out of my pockets, shouting at me and brandishing signs that had statements like, "Hands off the fluff" and "Bunnies aren't for pocket accessories."

Communication is an essential milestone in childhood development. In the United States for instance, there are certain language goals for children to meet. A guide of seeing where your child is at, compared to the majority and what they are capable of. Every child develops at different rates, which there are no objections to. However, I was not hitting many milestones, including not being able to verbalize 400+ words by the time I was 5 years old.

All I would do was point at the object or picture, regardless of the many cues that were presented to me. I was perhaps able to vocalize 40 words in total. Early on in my elementary school days, my speech issues could no longer be ignored. It wasn't a matter of months worth of communication delays. At least my parents didn't have to deal with a screaming child saying, "No!" or "Mine!" the whole time. I would point and cry, but that was about as far as I went. Every kid develops at different speeds and hits their milestones at various points. But no matter how hard I tried, I couldn't communicate in a way that the other kids could understand.

Every year, I would stand up as I was told to, trying to think in my head of what to say and how to say it.

Silently as I stood, the kids began to murmur and laugh. Quickly, I would sit down and bury my head onto my desk. I was labeled and stamped with the IEP plan early on in Kindergarten. A speech therapist had to come to my home to evaluate my delays and make a plan for me. I don't remember this interaction, but I would imagine hiding under some of my stuffed animals at the thought of an unknown person inside my house. This was when I got my first label.

My Speech/Language issues included (Warning Label):

Articulation Disorder: An individual with this disorder will have difficulty speaking words correctly. For example, individuals may not be able to produce the "R" sound and may struggle with forming the vocalization behind the "R," similar to Elmer Fudd's "I'm chasing Wabbits." This type of speech disorder can cause problems in producing sounds in syllables. So a perfect setup for making up my own language. Yay! Can I sign up to be a spy yet? I have my own unique style and repetitive noises ready, as I would avoid words that were difficult for me to say (except in my speech classes). Here I was forced to work through the vocals and sound everything out.

Cognitive-communication language disorder: Difficulty in Communication skills that involve memory, perception, and more. When children get put on IEP plans, it may or may not be noticeable, depending on the severity of the symptoms. Some children may have minor needs, like needing extra time on a test. For me, my IEP plan was anything but simple. I was taken out of class three times a week for extensive speech classes with two other kids. Little did I know that one of the kids in my IEP class, Erik, would become one of my best friends.

My comprehension difficulties did not at all help my anxiety. My parents had to constantly check-in with my teachers, including frequent phone calls home. I would assume the absolute worst every time and be filled with uncontrollable worry and anxiousness. Even if the teacher was calling to praise me, the simple line of "I'm calling your parents" would send me down a narrow and scary tunnel vision of panic. God dipped me in happiness and "anxious awareness" jelly and said, "WELP. Good luck."

While I struggled in school, my brother was the complete opposite of me. He strived and moved up in higher level classes for History, Math and Science, going through the same elementary school, with the same teachers. They often have this idea that you'll be like your sibling. Teachers would save my brother's paperwork for examples, and then in turn expect me to read my brother's work out loud. I struggled in all realms of education; I was a "C" student at best during elementary school.

Human beings, even as young children, tend to be judged if their verbal communication isn't up to par. Interactions and treatment tend to be different, positively or negatively. Some individuals might have better ways of communicating outside of being verbal. Many of them are judged if they have to go through Special Education for one thing or another.

Why does one kid in my class get to take the test by himself and have an extended 20 minutes? Some kids' IEP plans requires them to have the questions read out loud to them. Especially when the child may have a hard time comprehending the context. I was one of those students. Not only was I taken out of class several times a week to go through my speech classes, they also took me out during test time. I remember being placed in a small room with a few other students while the teacher read each question out loud. For multiple-choice questions, I would take my folder and cover up most of the answers, so I only saw one choice at a time. Otherwise, I would get overwhelmed at the four choices.

As a kid, I always kept my head down and tried not to stand out in the crowd. However, bullies always tended to creep through the hallways and scope out anyone they could pick on. Although I was bullied by kids my own age in elementary school, I also had a next-door neighbor named Willie. Willie was several years older than me but took a special interest in making fun of me, the awkward little girl in the cul-de-sac.

At first, I brought my Beanie Babies outside to play, imagining stories involving a family and a monkey and a lion. The bully would walk by, grab one or two of them, and throw them onto the rim of the basketball hoop, which he followed up with statements like "brat" and "useless, aren't you?" It got to the point where I wasn't allowed to play by myself outside because of the bullying. They had tried talking to Willie's parents, but to them their son could do no wrong.

My brother always had to accompany me if I was outside. He would play with me for a while, but then run off with his friends, forcing me to go back inside our house.

Willie's bullying Grand Finale took place when I was in 5th grade. I was walking across the street to pick up my brother from his friend's house for dinner. I wanted to bug him as part of my little sister duties. However, once I crossed the street I began to hear footsteps behind me. Before I could turn around I felt someone's hand grip the back of my neck. Next thing I knew my feet were lifted off the ground, as Willie choked slammed me to the ground. Facing the blue sky, I could hear Willie's laughter, which felt like it went on forever. I blinked a few times, realizing I was on the ground and having a difficult time catching my breath. I could hear my brother telling me to get up. He ended up helping me up and telling me to go home. There was redness around my neck from Willie's grip, as well as evidence from my brother and his friend. They both recounted Willie lifting my tiny body off the ground and then choke-slamming me. Hard.

Perhaps, he saw his target practice simply walk by like a hunter trying to bag a deer. I ran home, crying, shaking, filled with so much fear and confusion. I could barely get the words out to explain what had happened. I just kept crying, saying, "I'm hurt. I'm hurting." My dad checked me over and stormed out of the house to confront Willie. My brother had already punched him once or twice. Everything was kind of blurry after that. I know my dad went to Willie's house and told his parents exactly what had happened. After the chokeslam, I did not see Willie again. Perhaps they sent him away somewhere, or maybe they were worried about my parents taking further action. Months passed, and we ended up moving away—only 15 minutes from our previous house. But it was far enough to be in a completely different school district. The bullies were just as bad as the ones at my previous school. But at least this time, I didn't have one next door who apparently wanted to be a wrestler. It was a pretty effective chokeslam, I have to admit.

However, I wasn't exactly a great opponent at the age of 10, compared to a 14-year-old. People tend to fear and not understand someone different. Just because someone cannot talk well, does not mean they don't know what's going on. Simply put, just because someone smiles all the time does not mean they have everything perfectly aligned in their life. My start-up point in my education had to be backtracked due to my speech, language, and learning delays. It took me years of struggling and understanding how to make sense of the world. I ended up loving to read, even if at a slower pace. Judgments based on differences such as "they talk funny" or "they look different" can be toxic. How different would the world be if we accepted each other's differences?

CHAPTER 2:
Hello Grandparents!

Nearly every summer, my brother and I would take a break away from each other. Well, my parents would also benefit from only having one kid at the house versus two. Perhaps that was the main goal. Regardless, my brother and I would spend part of our summer in a small town near Peoria, Illinois. We would each have two weeks away from our parents and our other sibling to be with our grandparents. Both sides of our grandparents lived a block away from each other.

The population of their small town was around 600, including the chickens and the cows. There are some upsides and downsides of living in the middle of nowhere. There were comparable differences between a small-town community vs. a bigger city such as Naperville. For one thing, in downtown Naperville, there are way too many people walking and texting while crossing the street. I mean seriously, that's just asking to walk straight into someone's car, trip, and break a leg somehow. My clumsy radar always goes off for people in those situations—why ask for an accident? I would have walked into a store and knocked over a mannequin by now if I was one of those people who seemed to think multitasking equaled safety when walking, texting, chewing gum, and drinking.

The many differences between a small town vs. a city include but are not limited to:

1) Community: Living in a city consists of avoiding eye contact like the plague when it comes to strangers. Outside of having social anxiety, I mean. In smaller towns, you know everyone. Imagine having 20 houses surrounding you, knowing every single thing about your neighbors. You even know the darn fish's name that was flushed down the toilet the other day.

2) Smaller towns tend to be more closely knitted together because if you burn a bridge with one person, you're pretty much screwed out of a lot of jobs in the area. I mean, there's not even a grocery store. You have to actually go to a gas station for milk, eggs, and bread. Otherwise, you need to drive 30 minutes outside of town just to find a general grocery store.

3) Did I mention the annoying factor of small town living that everyone knows everyone? I mean, if you're even walking down the street and not really wanting to engage in conversation, you're still inviting everyone to flock to you and claim they know your mother and father—*and* your dog.

As a kid, I would walk a block to the gas station to grab milk for my grandma. I took every chance I could to be an adult and try to be more confident. My grandmother would give me enough money for milk, bread, and a small snack for myself. The first time I walked down the street, no one was outside. A couple cars drove by and I confidently made my way to the store. A car randomly stopped beside me and asked, "Hey, your XX Chromosome and XY Chromosome's kid right?" My fear radar went from 0-100 because a stranger talked directly to me and knew my parents. I ran straight back to my grandmother's house, which was probably a bad idea. The unknown man would know exactly where I was going then if he knew my parents. I ran inside and locked the door in a panic. Another odd thing with many small towns; you can just walk into someone's house like it's nothing.

There is no such thing as strangers in a small-town community. My grandmother stepped out of the kitchen and asked what happened. Before I could tell her there was a knock at the door. My grandmother told me to step away from the door, but I shook my head vigorously no. Then, as she opened the door, I hid behind her and sent the man dirty looks. In my head, I was kicking his ass, sending vibes of, "if you do anything, I'll kill you." The guy and my grandmother were talking like nothing had happened. And to them, nothing had happened. Just a small town neighbor saying hello and making conversation.

He apologized for scaring me—I'm sure I claimed I wasn't scared at all. He also mentioned that he remembered when I was just five years old, and knew my parents from years back. The man left and my grandmother said we could wait until tomorrow to go to the store. Mission Independent: Fail.

The next day, my mother called to check up on me and see how my vacation away from home was going. She also gave me an update on Annie, my stubborn, brown, chunky little hamster that didn't like to be touched. Immediately, I knew.

"She died, didn't she? I knew it! She's dead."

Mom had to calm me down, stating that my hamster was very much alive, and in fact, had babies.

According to my mom, my response was simply, "Why would she do that?"

Right? Why would a stubborn hamster who didn't like physical contact decide to have children? How dare she. As if my kid brain thought it was an automatic choice of the body to have kids overnight. Thank goodness it's not. Know how many pregnancy dreams I've had later in life? I would hate to randomly have one come true overnight. The next few days, my grandmother and I went over some possible names for the babies. The names were simple, such as Fluffy, Cutie, Sammy and Alex.

The next day I visited my other grandparents' house. This involved the typical burned hot dog and beans kind of a meal. I would scrape off the burned part of the hotdog and then they would take it away from me because I was wasting food by not eating the burned parts. Usually the same things happened when I would stay with my grandparents in the middle of nowhere. Both had different approaches to life. My mom's mom would often say I was rude, stupid, and other not-so-nice comments due to my speech delays and silences. She would oftentimes give me a piece of paper and expect me to entertain myself with it, since I had nothing else "going on up in there." After a few days, she would invite a few of my cousins to come over and bake cookies, rent movies, and more. She treated me as an equal in a way, when others were around. Or maybe she knew I was socially anxious and was hoping to make me "snap out of it." Regardless, that's how things were up until middle school when I stopped staying there for a few weeks each summer. Oh, and those who haven't had hamsters before, mom hamsters will sometimes eat the babies because her hormones are all out of whack and she thinks that by eating her young, she will be younger.

P.S. please don't ever take motherly advice from a hamster.

CHAPTER 3:
The Move

My family and I moved away from our small ranch house on the cul-de-sac when I was in middle school. I was transitioning to a new school, while my brother, within the first week of high school, decided he could do better at home. So my parents signed him up for online schooling while I was stuck attempting to socialize. I asked my parents if I could stay home as well, but because I still needed to see a speech therapist three times a week online learning wasn't doable at the time. Plus, it was going to be good for me to learn how to interact with people. Apparently.

Education is weird; the typical thing that parents tell kids is to not talk to strangers. But in an educational setting, it's completely okay and even encouraged. Talk to all the strangers you want while you're at school. Also, anything you do or say will be blown out of proportion and turned into a kids' crazy idea of a rumor. If it was a school full of random dogs, cats, and goats—that's a different story. I would talk to all the animal strangers, and it would be great. Unfortunately, I didn't go to a school full of animals (except for a few students). Then again, that's an insult to animals.

My mom came with me to pick up my schedule and check out the new school I would go to. I went too, as the middle school was newly built and it was time to find my locker. Walking down the filled hallways I was taken back to my previous school. I only had a friend or two in elementary school, but still I missed seeing familiar faces—even though I hardly talked to anyone. Making my way to my locker, I could already tell many people already knew each other. This would not be fair: new place, new speech therapist. I was not a fan of the new school. Not even a little.

I found my locker and looked up at my mom, merely stating, "Okay, I found it. Let's go."

My mom, with much patience, perhaps from always noticing how nervous I was with anything new, said, "don't you want to make sure you can open it? That way, you won't have any issues on your first day."

I suppose it made logical sense to make sure everything was in order before we left so I didn't randomly get anxious and want to show up thirty minutes before class to make sure. My mom knew how my mind worked more often than I wanted to admit. So I quickly checked and repeated the combination numbers to my mom to ensure that I remembered them. She went down the list with my school schedule and wanted to meet every single teacher. I shook my head, protesting—I didn't want to meet anyone.

I just wanted to go home and finish my book. Although I read very slowly, I still enjoyed reading. Even though my mom had zero interest in the fantasy books I read, she would always ask me what was happening in them. I suppose that was also to help with my communication skills.

I sighed as we made our way down the hallway. So much noise and chatter. It seemed like everyone was scrambling to meet everyone else. Just as we turned the corner, I thought I heard someone say my name. In front of me was someone I knew—a kid who was in my speech therapy class. Although I didn't know it at the time, he had Aspergers. Aspergers is a condition on the Autism spectrum. I never thought he was different though. I just thought he was quiet. And brilliant.

He moved away two years prior, and I lost his contact information. I could not help but smile.

"Erik?" I said, uncertain.

Even back then, I was always so anxious about mistaking someone for someone else. He nodded, and we said hello once more before walking away in opposite directions. That was how our friendship was. We were in speech therapy together for years. We spoke very little to each other, mostly when there was a crowd of other people around.

Both of us got worked up, drained, and exhausted in social situations. Perhaps this is why we have always been so close, regardless of how far apart we were. It took a lot of time and trust for him to be okay with anyone hugging him. Little did we both know that I would become one of those people in his life that he was okay hugging. My mom looked down at me, hinting, wanting to know who he was.

"Mom, he was the only boy I invited to my birthday parties. That was Erik."

She nodded, trying to remember.

My mother always worked. I always respected her for it, even though I missed her at home. She was a nurse and would often work 60+ hours a week. However, when she was home she always made sure we knew we were loved.

My mother talked to each of my teachers and gave them a mini rundown of everything I needed. She told them that I had a hard time with change, that they may need to repeat their questions, and that I had an Individual Education Plan that they needed to follow. My mom had always been my advocate throughout my special education journey. My dad was as well, but my mother was much more outspoken. Plus, my father had mental health issues of his own that he was dealing with, so interacting with people was not something he especially wanted to do.

As the days went on, my anxiety began to build as the first day of school approached. My mom went around and told all the teachers my entire life story (well, more like a general map of what works for me).

She would casually embarrass me, saying things like, "Introduce yourself. Can you give your teacher a smile?"

No, no, I cannot, nor do I want to. I want to hide my face. Pretend I am a wizard and cast a spell to disappear. Can I do that? Disappear and find some dogs and cats to hold? Pretend they are my new classmates? I can better interact with animals, and this would help them become more sociable with people. A win-win!

However, the dreaded day dawned; not involving animals unfortunately. The first day at my new school, my mom brought up the fact that I knew someone from our previous school, which implied that I would have a great time. Perhaps they hoped my friend Erik would be in every class with me.

Maybe if I let her, she would have asked the principal to change my schedule. But they would have turned it down; Erik was in advanced classes in science and math. Pretty sure they wouldn't throw someone "below student average" into advanced courses. I clutched my Pokemon backpack as the bus pulled up. I told my parents I could handle myself and didn't need them to drive me to school. I didn't need them to walk me out of the car and wish me a good day. My dad hugged me, as though it was the last time. Being twelve years old at this point, I wanted to find my own way and assert my independence, starting with the dreaded 7th grade.

I took a deep breath, holding onto my Pokemon backpack as if this was the first step to something new. Perhaps a place where I wouldn't be made fun of. Maybe a place where I could pretend to be someone else while staying silent and observing everyone else. I would no longer be the awkward kid or the kid that cried randomly during class. I was going to make this work, even though everything was so triggering. The way the kid next to me chewed his gum—the chatter of everyone talking on the bus. The bus was a horror show. Why do people condemn themselves to be in a small space with twenty other people? As the bus headed towards the school, I felt as though I was going to puke. The crowd seemed to be getting louder. As my heart began to beat faster, I realized I had no idea what I was doing. All the new faces, the unknowns and uncertainty came rushing over me at once. Just as I felt light-headed, the bus stopped at the parking lot. People scrambled out of the bus, as the person next to me said, "move it!" breaking me out of my daydream.

I looked up at the brick building; I had been here the week before. My mom told me that was to be prepared so as not to get lost. However, I think that was a load of shit, as my anxiety was ramping up inside me. At the time I didn't know this; I thought it was just nervousness.

I made my way towards my locker, as if making sure it was still there. That a magical dragon didn't randomly take it and leave me in an awkward position of 'sorry, a dragon took my locker.' I wanted to make sure I knew exactly where it was and how long it would take to get to each of my classes. Making my way to the first classroom, I noticed many students standing in front of the school, lingering and talking among themselves. I made myself comfortable at the wall. I clenched onto one of my Pokemon books. I was not reading; I knew I could not concentrate with everyone around me. However, merely having something familiar made everything a bit...more comfortable to deal with. As though reading my mind, sensing how anxious I was feeling, a student asked me if I was new to the area. Technically, I was not. My previous school district was fifteen minutes away. Did that count as being from the area? Or did that mean I wasn't since it was a different district?

My brain continued on its pathway as I nervously just nodded my head. She nervously laughed and went back to her friends. Yep...I was making a great impression already.

I sighed and tried to think of a way to convince my parents to enroll me in online school. My dad was home for most of the day, sleeping for the majority of the time...maybe I could give him the motivation to help me. Yes! That was it; I could help with motivating him by helping me. That was how my brain always worked. I wanted to help my dad with everything he was going through, even though I did not know what was going through his mind.

Classes were... well... tedious and nerve-wracking. I could not imagine being a teacher and trying to get everyone to feel welcomed and yet understood. Every person was unique in what they could or could not handle. I always overthink. I never wanted to be the one to overwhelm someone. Regardless, the classes were filled with prompts like, "say your name and tell us about yourself." As much as I wished I could perform magic, I did not have any magical abilities in actual life, nor in tricking the mind. I always ended up casually stating that I had a cat and a dog and that I just moved.

Uninteresting, unlike the many overthinking thoughts that came through my mind. My ears would occasionally perk up with the mention of something interesting from my peers. Animals, anime, books, and well, anything that I could tell that they had a passion for. Everyone had a face on throughout the class; I felt the uncertainty of whom to trust and why. Gathering my books and keeping my eyes to the ground, I made my way to my last class. So far, I had not been bullied, so I supposed that was a success. I sighed in anticipation of my art class. I did enjoy art class at my previous school. However, I was exhausted and yet had hardly spoken to anyone. I sat down at a random spot.

I took out one of my favorite iconic characters in the Pokemon world - Pikachu. The folder in black lettering at the upper right corner read "ART." I had everything organized and had my assignments per folder, to show my parents and to be aware of my homework assignments. They would check it every day, as usual, and make sure I checked everything off in my classes. Art was one of the few subjects that I wanted to get better at. It did not involve speaking as much as the other courses or putting thoughts into words and expressing ourselves through a unique form outside of words alone. I told my parents I would try to make a friend if Erik ended up not being in any of my classes—which he was not. I did casually raise my head to look around to see if I saw anyone familiar. Lost in my thoughts, I heard someone making their way over to me. I looked around and saw a few empty seats, and yet she sat right next to me. Perhaps she did not know anyone here as well? She shuffled through her backpack, looking for her folder. I remember biting my lip and remembering the promise I had made to my parents to try and make a friend. I nervously looked over at her and thought I would say "Hello" and wipe it off as a mission complete; I tried. What came out was not a normal greeting.

As she placed her folder on the desk, I looked at her with serious eyes and asked, "Do you like Pokemon?"

Before she could even answer, my mind was already pushing back at me with many stupid thoughts of how I had just messed up. But without judgment, the girl nodded her head and said, "I have watched a few episodes." And she left it at that.

I kept going, ignoring my overthinking thoughts and self-doubt. This girl listened to my talk of Pokemon for the last minute or two before class started. I do not know what came over me; I was so nervous that I could not stop talking incredibly fast. I chose her to be the first person with whom I interacted. I suppose the Pokemon reference of "I choose you!" was quite fitting. Little did I realize that she would become one of my best friends. She accepted my oddness, timidness, and my whole bundle of awkwardness.

After art class, we started talking about our little obsessions. I'm not sure how we came up with random topics, but everything just kind of flowed into place. We both realized that we lived about a block away from each other, and she had recently moved from Puerto Rico about two years prior. She was still shy with most people, and we started talking little by little after school on the telephone. Everything seemed to be going well, right? New friend, reconnecting with my elementary school friend, adjusting slowly to the changes of a new school. Perhaps, I was just lying to myself, or I did not realize what exactly I was feeling. There were times I wanted to cry for no reason. Where I felt uncomfortably numb to the point of feeling like I didn't exist.

Perhaps, the depression had always been there, hiding in place. But when the beast appeared it didn't introduce itself. It was a part of me, standing awkwardly at my side not really saying anything. When the beast appeared, there was no sudden use of a magic wand or statement saying, "You will be sad now." Instead, it sat there in the corner of my mind. Spouting terrible things towards me throughout the day. Linking its very body to my heart in order to have everything seem so heavy and out of place. I couldn't even put into words how I was feeling or why. I would still laugh as I hung out with my friend Lisa. But then there would be plenty of times that I felt drained and withdrawn. When I did not want to talk to anyone for days. The beast was becoming more and more apparent and sitting heavily on my very soul.

CHAPTER 4:
The Beast Within

The beast stared with much gratitude. Words of lies posted as truths. Tainting the mind with notes of repetitive emotions and thoughts. The beast, living within many of us. An all too familiar and yet very different creature that tortures for fun. Although the beast may bring friends, just for the fun of it. Add in doubts, insecurities, and the pain that follows. Yet, those that are connected and acknowledge the beast may find those that understand the beasts inside themselves and fight alongside you. Developing relationships with those that you may not have thought possible. They can be a reason worth living for, to continue finding that light source and people to help. The friends we make along the way help put layers of protection upon our shields. To better protect and to serve, our general tribe of those that have fought monsters before.

One of the most harmful mental games we can play is called "comparison." The thoughts of wanting to be where everyone else seems to be at. Truth be told, every flower blooms differently. The different soil, exposure to sunshine and water is different. Would a gardener give the same amount of water to a sunflower as they do to a flock of daisies? Comparison dismisses an individual path. There is a difference between "What can I do today to be better?" versus "My best friend has their whole life together. What am I doing wrong?"

Why is this so harmful? Because in the process we are devaluing who we are as a person, including our starting points, our experiences and our circumstances, all because we are comparing ourselves to someone else that isn't us. It's one thing to have a goal, but it's another to belittle yourself in the process. There are hundreds and thousands of different books in the same genre. Different perspectives of the same general story.

For example, girl meets guy and finds out he is a vampire that is afraid of dogs. Three different people will write the story differently. Their perspective on the characters, the type of characters, the direction the story goes in are all unique. Even with that simple line for a story: "Girl falls in love with a vampire who fears dogs." That's the same thing that goes on with life. Each person is unique in their gifts, starting points, circumstances, etc. Just because you aren't the top Sales Representative in your company, doesn't mean you aren't good. There might be something that works for them in their tactics, but not for you. Or better yet, you may need to find your own pen and write your own successful story.

Write, scratch off and continue on until you get something good for yourself. Every book is different—every fantasy, sci fi book and romance can be different and yet the same. That doesn't mean we should burn every single book that isn't a popular choice among our peers. There are plenty of amazing books out there that haven't broken through for one reason or another. By tainting our own story and comparing others negatively to ourselves, we are initially disregarding the pages we have written thus far. That isn't fair to ourselves at all. Not after everything we have been through to get here. Acknowledging where we are now, even with messy handwriting, is one of the most beautiful and joyful things in life. We have lived, and therefore we have continued our story to move on to the next part. The thoughts of "We shouldn't feel depressed or anxious because A,B, C person has it so much worse." You owe it to yourself to accept and acknowledge your emotions as your own. Comparing yourself is slowly destroying and discouraging your growth, self-love and self-care. Just because someone else may have it "worse" doesn't mean you shouldn't feel sad about what life is throwing at you. If your brain decides to have a freakout, that's okay. You are here to continue on your own path.

"People who are dealing with depression, addiction, suicidal thoughts, or mental illness... They're strong. You're strong because you've been in this fight and you wake up thinking you're going to beat it again today."

Jared Padalecki (Supernatural Actor)

CHAPTER 5:
High School Adventures and Doctors

Ligh school is the best and most important part of life! It's a great way to meet new friends, discover new hobbies and take over the world with zombie llamas chewing on fruit cake. Said no one ever. Well, except for, I suppose, individuals that ended up liking high school, or perhaps believe "It was the best part of their life." But perhaps these people are zombies from the future that created a way to come back and live off their high school days again...because they are already dead on the inside and outside.

Oswego, IL was growing rapidly when I was in middle school. The town had a large population and built another high school. The only cool thing I remember being a part of in middle school was voting for the new high school's mascot and colors. I wanted Wolves, and it needed to match the mascot, so silver and blue was the best bet. This was the only thing that I liked about high school, that I voted correctly, and somehow, the mass majority were in sync with having Wolves being a badass mascot with silver and blue as our color. Otherwise...high school sucked.

I went to high school with all the same kids I was with in 7th and 8th grade, so I had no opportunity to redefine myself. Going to a new school, I already had the labels of "Pokemon nerd," "ugly girl," and "mute girl." I wasn't really mute. I just chose to only talk to a handful of people, when and if I became comfortable with them.

I was still working through my speech therapy issues—I had gotten better since elementary school. No longer did I make up my own language of noises, and I was able to verbalize my thoughts—If I chose to. Instead, I was labeled as shy, ugly and well...I am sure there were more labels than those. I kept my head down and did my absolutely best not to stick out from the crowd.

These were the same kids who noticed that I always kept my head down in the hallways and avoided human interaction. However, when someone was part of my friend group, I protected them and always made sure they were okay above all else. I showed my goofy and nerdy side instead of my quiet exterior—no longer in fear of judgment or afraid to say the wrong thing.

Days before high school started, I was standing outside the school after receiving my class schedule. The most important thing was comparing schedules with my best friend, Lisa, and a handful of people that I actually got along with throughout middle school. None of them were in my classes. Erik had advanced classes and was no longer a special ed student like myself. While he was still on an IEP plan, he was also someone who was really smart and could absorb anything like a sponge, one of the many things I wish I had the ability to do. None of my friends were in my classes—they weren't even in the same lunch period I was in. I legit had no one that I knew walking in on my first day. For our first day of high school, Lisa and I decided it would be best to no longer use the bus. We both wanted to avoid being stuck on it again, with all the bullying. Lisa's mom offered to drive us to school every morning, and my dad would help as well. We both did not want to engage in the social nonsense of bullying.

Regardless, we followed each other to our lockers on the opposite sides of the hallway. We hugged as though we knew that this was going to be a forever battle for each of us. She was just as nervous about new surroundings as I was. We gave each other our schedules, so if we had time one of us would race down the hallway to see the other before our next class. Me being an anxious person, nervous about being late to anything, she knew I wanted to be in my next class a minute or two early. The utter thought of being the last one in the classroom absolutely terrified me.

Lunch time was absolutely one of the worst things ever. At least in the classroom, all you had to worry about was finding your name and hope that you sat next to someone who was quiet and kept to themselves. Lunch was a whole other story. There weren't assigned seats. Instead, it was a question of who you could sit with and introduce yourself to. No one I knew was in the room—the select few that I had become friends with were in their classes learning, while I was there awkwardly standing around trying to find a place to sit. My heart beat faster and faster at the anticipation of standing there, looking like I did not belong.

I began feeling light-headed and ran into the bathroom and locked myself in the stall. No noises, just quiet. I clenched my backpack onto my lap and sat in the stall. Just relax, I told myself—as if that would solve all the problems in the world. If only our own positive voice always overtook the negative side of our self-talk. I looked at my watch and told myself I would stay there until a few minutes before my next class and would try again tomorrow. Once a week, I would have my speech therapy class—they assigned me to a special ed teacher who would be in each of my classes throughout. This made nothing go by that much easier. She was someone new in my life circle. I missed my elementary school speech pathologist. I had the same teacher for 5 years, and nothing changed until she moved, causing my life to spin out of control dealing with the changes. Regardless, here I was in the bathroom stall with no one to talk to.

The following class was English, a subject that I would always struggle with. It had always been difficult to put my thoughts into words and make them understandable. Those that can read can alternate between different writing styles. A writer can write about the red drapes on the window and have them symbolize anguish, making the reader feel anguish throughout the story.

I took out my folder, looking around, hoping that Lisa would pop out of nowhere to tell me they changed her class. Of course, that wouldn't make sense since she had her English class with a different teacher in the morning. Little did I know this teacher would change my life. She encouraged each of us to keep a journal and write daily. Regardless if it was about life, thoughts, or anything else. She wanted us to experiment with our writing voice and have us find out what we actually enjoyed writing about. I found myself wanting to write outside of class, even if I wanted to try to write a specific type of poem. Mrs. Scapino, my English teacher, became the first person that I ever showed my poetry to. I wanted her opinion on my writing to become a better writer. I wanted to explore and find more writing material to read and to relate to. I wanted to find and build up my writing voice through her. That would happen later, however, when I became comfortable showing her my work.

The next day during English class, we made our way to the library to get our library cards and my free access to the heaven of books. Our teacher wanted us to rent out a book of our choosing, while we also picked up the first book for our reading section of the class. I went up and down the many books and came to realize that the library could be my new place during lunch. I picked up a poetry book about dogs and a fantasy book by Mercedes Lackey that I wanted to try to get into. I checked off my book and nervously asked the librarian if I could be there during my lunch... After a little thought, the librarian decided it was allowed. It meant the world to me that I would not sit in the bathroom stall—alone.

The library became an escape for me, as I would rent out books and be alone throughout. I could not bring myself to tell Lisa that I had been switching between sitting in the bathroom or the library. She said she met a new friend during her Spanish class, and they had been eating lunch together with a few of her classmate's friends. I would smile as I told her I had been reading more, but not by myself. I didn't want her to worry about me, I didn't even want to worry about myself. I did not want to face the kind of judgement I felt when I was surrounded by people. At times I couldn't even bring myself to go to the library. Sometimes I would hide in the bathroom and cry for no reason at all. Feeling so overwhelmed that I could not even identify what was going on.

I was still being shoved at school, getting slapped on the back of my head by bullies who thought I was too strange. Everything was the same in this regard, but I was feeling like I was losing myself bit by bit. Piece by piece, a part of me would break off and find its way into the trash. I couldn't even concentrate on books anymore. Although, I had dabbled with writing poetry and short stories in my free time. I could not concentrate on the words I wanted to say, nor could I concentrate on the words written in stories I wanted to escape into. My mind was filled with thoughts of worthlessness, and yet... I didn't even know how I could put those feelings into words. Or if I would even want to speak of them. Everything was becoming foggy as I detached myself from things I was interested in. I talked to my friends less and less as I got pushed and stomped on at school with little thought. Perhaps it was the only time I actually felt pain versus the numbness my body was used to.

Little by little, without realizing it, I was eating less and less, even outside of the school. I would come home and see my dad asleep on the couch, while my brother was locked in his room, ignoring the world. There would be times on occasion where I would knock on his bedroom door and ask to hangout with him. At this point, my brother was doing his online classes and was trying his best to graduate early. His end goal was to leave the house as soon as possible so he could get away from us. He had shut the world down, and little did I know at the time, he was also battling his own depression. I did not want to bother him or anyone else again. I began to feel as though I was an inconvenience. My preferred food throughout the day was a granola bar, an apple, and perhaps a bowl of cereal. My home life was never normal; my dad dealt with depression daily. Going undiagnosed, there were times where he would sleep all day without making a noise. I often would come home and see him passed out on the couch. I would stand there and make sure he was breathing and then make my way up the stairs. It wasn't always like this.

Sometimes we would watch anime together after I got my homework done. Sometimes we would go out and buy random movies and watch them. But there were also times where my dad did not have the energy to interact with anyone. My dad had not worked in 20+ years. As a kid, I always got defensive by how my friend's parents would react when I would tell them my dad was a stay-at-home parent. My mom was a nurse that worked many hours a week; 60+ hours a week was not an abnormal amount of hours for a nurse. My father was just always there. I thought nothing of it. I thought he was always extra-tired and overwhelmed, just as I was. I made my way up the stairs, trying to be as quiet as I could to ensure I did not wake him up, and I was never sure if I would get my loving father or the person who got irritated with everything.

Sometimes emotions can be so overwhelming that we do not even know what or how we are feeling. In the day-to-day life of being a teenager, we may not even realize what is or is not normal. Little by little, I felt I had no energy to shower, let alone dress. I would throw on my favorite hoodie that I had worn a few times before and keep going. I found myself less and less in the library during lunch. More often than not I locked myself in the bathroom stall after being pushed against my locker once more. My very existence was frozen, and there was no point of even breathing—but I continued on. I stopped taking care of myself from showering, homework, and more.

My mom took notice of my matted hair and would wake me up early after sleeping just a few hours before work and toss me in the shower. She didn't think much of my recent weight loss, nor my lack of energy. Then again, I had always been a tiny girl—heck, I didn't even notice how my clothes felt looser on my slim frame. I was just going day by day and working on surviving and not breaking down. I enjoyed nothing as much as I used to; I lost interest in even listening to my friend's stories of her day. I tried to concentrate on anything other than my inner dialogue of thoughts. But I was unsuccessful.

One day, I woke up in a panic, feeling like it was hard to breathe. I ran to the bathroom, splashed water on my face, and tried to cool down. When that didn't work, I thought about the Pokemon theme song to try and get my breathing under control. I looked in the mirror, as though for the first time. I noticed the indents on my skin and how my body had changed over the past few months. I grabbed the scale from the bathroom which I had never used. I had always been slim, but something told me I needed to check. In a matter of eight months from my last doctor's appointment, I had lost 20 pounds—without trying. 20 pounds gone from hardly feeling enough energy to eat. I took a step back and weighed myself again. As though a magical unicorn would pop up and say, "Just kidding! Let's make your life brighter." I stared at the numbers... I was under 80 pounds. That didn't seem right; nothing about this seemed right. Walking into the bedroom, I knew something was not right for me. How long had it been like this?

I made my way downstairs. My dad was eating his breakfast with a smile on his face. Thank goodness he was not fighting his own beast that day—or perhaps he was hiding it. I took a deep breath, unsure of what future events would bring. I sat down next to my dad ands prepared to speak. But instead of the words I had rehearsed inside my head for the past few minutes, tears came and I was unable to speak any further. My dad hugged me, unsure what was going on. I looked at him with those eyes of concern that have seen all the battles that life brings those who are fighting depression. I ended up stating I needed help. My dad immediately called my mom while she was at work. I pleaded with him not to call, telling him it could wait until she got home, that I would stay up and wait for her. I kept pleading—perhaps in fear or anticipation of what was to come.

My dad had undiagnosed depression which would later cause him to experience cabin fever. Cabin fever is not a specific diagnosis: it's a constellation (yes, like the stars in the sky) of symptoms that occur when someone is isolated for long periods of time. He had his own cocktail of issues that he had been bottling up for years. He would get worried about other people's motives and thus lock himself away. Throughout my life, I had seen him calling my mom's work and making sure she was okay. Making sure she was still at work because she didn't call him to let him know she was on her way. I never thought of him as someone who was controlling. But he was so nervous, thinking that if he didn't call one day something horrible would happen.

"Your daughter wants to talk to you. Are you free?"

I didn't know how much my dad was fighting his own monsters—I didn't think any one of us wanted to admit it. Regardless, my dad went to call my mom. My mom got irritated that he was calling her again during her workday. She did not know; no one could have. My dad handed the phone over to me and I think everything broke in our perfect glasshouse, of trying to have everything seem normal to the outside world. I cried and told my mom I needed help. I couldn't even muster how to even say it or why.

My mom took off work early, and we went to the doctor. I was sitting there in the all-white room, with the doctor staring at the paper, going one by one through the questions. I looked at my mom and noticed that she and my dad were bickering on the side of the room. I caught notes of "Whose fault is this?" and "Why didn't you notice?" I wanted to crawl into a hole and not have anyone worry about me ever again. I remember that feeling all too well.

I went through the typical questions that the doctor would ask me, "Does anything hurt?" Everything—I wanted to say.

"Have you lost interest in your normal activities—Yes! I get easily distracted; that is normal. But I can't bring myself to even read or attempt writing. I had no interest in my only few escapes from life. But I shrugged my shoulders. He was concerned and talked to my parents about early-onset osteoporosis. I sat there, feeling at a loss of control. Waiting and wanting some miracle of all my monsters sitting next to me to magically go away. But I felt as though I was slowly being choked, released, and then choked once more when I thought things would get better soon. The monsters liked to tease—they always did. The doctor suggested that I should see a specialist and a nutritionist.

The car ride to the psychiatric ward was deafening. My parents thought I might have an eating disorder, but I just fell silent, shaking my head and quietly protesting. I always had an interest in psychology and health. Yet I couldn't see that I was falling into grips of depression. You never think it'll happen to you. No matter how much you understand depression, the beast comes out whether or not something is going on.

Then we went to a small building outside of the major hospital. There, a doctor asked me some questions with my parents in the room, and then had my parents leave to ask some more questions. She asked more of the same mental health questions. Did I feel suicidal? No, and that was the truth. How long do these emotions last? On and off but can last days or perhaps weeks. But they are getting more severe. I was absolutely nervous to even mention that it really upset me for no reason at all. They put me on an outpatient plan. I did not need to stay at the psych ward. Rather, I needed to see a psychologist twice a week and a nutritionist once a week to get my weight back up. Let the 6-month plan begin.

Nervous on the first day was an absolute understatement. I did not understand what to say or where to begin. How does one even talk about their thoughts if they do not even know where to start? Or why did it start in the first place? The psychologist went through the eating disorder questions again during our visits. Making sure I was comfortable getting back to a normal weight while eating healthy. And asking questions pertaining to my depression. I did not trust her; I underplayed my depression by a lot, telling her I felt sad and tired most of the time. But I did not talk about the negative thoughts, the numbing emotions, feeling overwhelmed, irritated, or not wanting to eat despite logically knowing that I needed to.

After a few months, I was feeling open. We got to a plan of writing my emotions down and any thoughts I wanted to speak about. Honestly, that helped for the time being. It was one of the many reasons I got into poetry. I started looking up poems and identifying other writers' works as: "This is what I want to say! This is me. How can I say it as well?" and went on from there.

After many sessions, we moved my psychologist to once a month while I kept seeing my nutritionist consistently. I was about fifteen years old and graduated from not having to see my psychologist again. All in all, I had seen my psychologist for a year. Well, I shouldn't say I graduated as if we had a huge ceremony. More like my parents had a copy of her number and hung it up on the fridge as a daily reminder that I had someone to talk to, and everything was perfect. They never asked me what happened during those sessions or what we talked about. I was glad for that; I was glad for the actual privacy of the matter, even if I did not tell my psychologist everything. I did not talk about my dad's depression, for one. Nor did I mention the bullying or the anxiety that came when I was in crowds. I barely touched the surface of what I was experiencing. I told her I felt nervous with tests, just as most people do. I did not tell her that at times I got tunnel vision and my heart felt as if it was going to pop out of my chest. I did not tell her how nervous I was with simply being with people. I just told her I was shy and kept to myself. In regards to my dad's depression, I do not think I wanted to talk about it, or acknowledge that my dad's beasts existed. I don't think I could have bared to have her possibly tell him I told him about it, and that I was aware of it. The last thing I wanted to do was have him blame himself, which I know for a fact he would have. But this wasn't the reason. It could have been multiple things at once or my brain playing games and seeing if I would survive. Truth be told, my ever growing depression could have built up without the outside influence of school or my parents. I was simply depressed, and had no energy. Our minds can be our own worst enemy as we go through this weird cycle called life.

The Bringer

The beast enters in unexpectedly.

Bringing in words of false perceptions,

Surrounding thyself with negative climate

In an attempt to drown the very soul in torment.

Draining the very energy of life

Replacing such light with darkness.

Only to continue being misunderstood,

By those around internally and externally.

Wishing to scream the feelings away,

Only to realize the emptiness of energy left.

Comparison and false reflection

Second nature in a scrambled mind.

Keeping hope close for a better day,

Touching internally in self-care and restfulness

A continuous warrior in the fight,

Against internal demons that surround.

"Life can only be understood backward, but it must be lived forwards."

Søren Kierkegaard

CHAPTER 6:
Highschool: Boobs are the Secret to a Man's Heart—Except Not really

Senior year of high school had finally come. The pressure was on figuring out what I wanted to do for the rest of my life. No big deal at all, really. No big deal. Just prepping for the ACTs and trying to figure out what career I wanted to get into... no big deal...at all. I made my way through the familiar doors, expecting to go to my first class. I turned the corner to a very crowded hallway. I missed the summer already; I kept in touch with some acquaintances throughout the summer and mostly hung out with Lisa. Now it was time to get back into school mode and go to my favorite class, English. Luckily, I had the same teacher as I always did for English class. English was the only class that I got an "A" in and it was also the class that got me comfortable sharing my poetry. Otherwise, I kept my poetry folder secret and always with me in my backpack. Just in case I ever wanted to write during lunch break or perhaps in the library.

Long gone were the days of sitting in the bathroom, but I'd still sit in the library and keep to myself. On one of these days, out of the corner of my eye I saw one of my acquaintances. I went to greet her when she exclaimed, "YOU HAVE BOOBS!"

I froze in place, gave her a look, and walked right into the bathroom. Right, I was no longer flat-chested. I stared at the mirror as though it was the first time. It wasn't as though I didn't notice before, but this time I regretted not wearing my favorite hoodie. I hit puberty way late, so boobs were the first thing anyone was going to see. Regardless, I made my way through the rest of the day. However, somehow, the few bullies I had in high school paid no attention to me. These boobs were great! Annoying and in the way, but I felt as though I was being seen...but when I really thought about it, it confirmed how much I disliked most people. Why is status determined by boobs anyways? Guys are strange...that is what I told myself.

My first boyfriend was a football player. Yeah, I wasn't expecting that either. He and I were acquaintances for a few years. He was a year younger than I was, but he was also an anime nerd like me. He asked me out of the blue, nervously; I said yes. And we went about our day. I went home and logged into my computer, and we talked about our favorite shows, and things seemed as familiar as anything. No changes, which is what I liked.

Suddenly, out of the blue, he asked, "When are we going to kiss?"

The very first thought in my head was, 'Why would anyone want to kiss on the first day of being together?' I didn't understand it. Shouldn't you get to know someone first, kiss later perhaps? Even then, kissing was...problematic. Kissing felt too intimate, and too unfamiliar. Perhaps it was due to my anxiety, or simply that I didn't like the idea of our lips touching.

I remember responding with, "Um...can we hold hands first tomorrow? And go from there?"

He went ignored me the next day. We only dated for a day, and were already having issues. Plus, he wasn't even communicating with me on what the heck was bothering him. I brushed it off as the pressure of an away game later that night. He knew I was not into sports, so I surprised my friend. We have known each other for two years and were dating for a day... so nothing weird about that. After school, I went to the store and bought a few things for him. I made a care package for his away game. Snacks, drinks, and one of our favorite books. Because after getting smacked around all night, who wouldn't want to read?

Although I already had my driver's license, my dad needed to borrow my car while his car was in the shop. We drove 45 minutes away after school, and he dropped me off and told me to call him when the game was close to ending, and he would be close by. I am sure to this day that he was expecting me to call him within fifteen minutes and say, "Get me away from all these people! Why am I allowing myself to be engaged in this torture?" The game dragged on, as I tried to stay engaged. I wanted to let my first boyfriend ever know that I was paying attention. Also, side note: Why the heck do football games not provide hot chocolate?

Seriously, why do people like to sit out in the cold freezing their tits off? I just got these boobs too, the last thing I wanted them to do was plop off awkwardly and run away.

After the game, I already saw him meeting up with some friends. I ran over with my care package and hugged him from behind. Ignoring the rest of the crowd, he turned around, and I handed him his care package.

He asked, "Why are you here?"

I told him he seemed down earlier and I wanted to surprise him. That was when his friend chimed in, "Oh, is she the one you're taking to the dance next month?"

With much coldness, he replied, "No."

I laughed it off because how else was I supposed to break the awkward tension? I hadn't even thought about the dance, I never went to those things, but this was a very odd second day of dating. I mean, I'd never dated anyone before, but this did not sit right with me. I pushed the basket to him again and apologized for bothering him.

We broke up the next day. He broke up with me, which I found out was because I admitted to him I was not comfortable kissing. Go figure! Guys are weird, that is what I told myself. I had crushes before, but if this was the drama I was going to be dealing with, perhaps I just wanted to stay single for the rest of my life.

So that is the story of how I dated a football player for two days. That has to be a record for failed dating tactics.

After a few weeks, my boobs lost their power. I was back to being bullied, just as I usually was. One semester, in the middle of 12th grade, I sat in the gym with my classmates. We were all in rows, sitting down alphabetically. I heard the usual teasing from a bully and gave him no eye contact. Next thing I knew, the guy decided it was a great idea to jump over me—his foot contacting directly to my head. I blacked out for a second, and sitting up, I remember glaring at him. I wanted so badly to lose it, scream and attack. But I held everything in. None of the teachers saw anything, and the rest of the students kept to themselves. Thus, I fell more and more silent, stuck in my head. Regardless of what anyone might say, the mind plays tricks on your self-worth—or lack of it.

Towards the end of high school, I dated again. Life is strange because we may find someone attractive no matter how many red flags fly up in the air. To others, it may seem that the room is getting moldy, with little cockroaches crawling about, while we sit happily in the filth, justifying the red flags and pretending flowers were growing from chocolate. I had a terrible streak choosing guys; spoiler alert, it does get better. But what is a story with no wrong turns?

My father and I had been going to church for the past few weeks. I grew up Catholic but after 10th grade my dad wanted me to choose whether I wanted to keep going to church, so that he knew he wasn't forcing it upon me. He wanted me to figure out how I wanted to engage with religion and if I wanted to continue. That, or he also wanted to avoid crowds as much as I did. However, I wanted to try something new, which was very abnormal for me as I usually followed a set pattern to keep my nerves at bay. Something came over me. I wanted to explore and be a rebel. Well...a rebel by my standards. The church was having an event for older teenagers/young adults. So guess who threw herself into a mob of Christians and hormones? This girl. I checked out the group and was dumbfounded, finding over thirty people in one room.

There was a band playing Christian rock throughout — and no, I did not start dating a band member. I ended up bumping into someone who knew I was new. I reeked of shyness, awkwardness and well... newness. Steve was his name, and he had blonde hair and blue eyes. He was lanky and nerdy — he was a computer hacker and video gamer. Yep, my weakness, even though I hardly know anything about hacking computers. But I had a fondness for nerds figuring out how things worked. We ended up talking and hung outside of the church group once a week. The church was enormous and had its own coffee shop. I would order hot chocolate, and we would chat about randomness—anything that came to mind. Best of all, he did not try or attempt physical contact. While I was 17, Steve was about 20 years old. I was developing a full on teenage crush on him—but I also did not want to ruin it with relationship junk.

Well, one thing led to another. With the way he slowly reached for my hand, his eyes asking for permission. After our many encounters, he had mentioned that he was broken. So was I! What a brilliant match made in heaven; that's all you need for a relationship, right? He told me up front that he had just gotten out of a breakup. That he was still in love with his ex and did not want to hurt me — but also wanted to be with me. How sweet and romantic ... the cockroaches were parading as we spoke, and all I could feel was the fact that someone didn't want to hurt me. I became his distraction, something that he could access when he felt depressed — and I allowed it.

My first kiss was from someone that imagined I was his previous lover. The way he would cuddle with me, only if I felt comfortable, was in hopes for comfort from the arms of someone that held his heart. Little by little, I lost myself, hoping I could get him to love me how he loved her. I tried to understand the cracks in his heart by being there for him. Even though he was not entirely into the relationship, I wanted to show him I would not leave him. Three out of the six months that we were together he left the country to volunteer.

While he was in Australia, he messaged me admitting he cheated on me several times. That he was crying out for his ex's name as he laid in the hospital bed, drunk, for many nights. I bit my lips and assured him I did not think any differently of him. That we would talk about everything when he got back. He was supposed to be around for prom. I wanted to bring him and go to a dance with a date. Lisa was already starting to date her boyfriend, and the last thing I wanted to do was be a third wheel. He said he would try to get tickets for the week before so he would be there. Three days before prom, he said he couldn't make it. He said he was stuck for another week or two. But I saw he posted a picture on Facebook with him and his ex. He could go back...to see her. Not to see me, when I thought he was mine. I told my friend I didn't want to go to a stupid dance and told my parents I was not going because I was not feeling myself.

The day after prom, Steve ended up moving to California and leaving me a special note to remember him by:

"If I met you before Katie, I would have loved you."

That was just what I wanted to hear, from someone I thought I loved and cared for. That my timing was off with my very existence.

Trying to put Steve in the past, I thought graduating high school would be the best. An opportunity to no longer make mistakes. Side note: I was still naïve to the core. I was going to focus on school. ACTs kicked my ass regarding getting into college. It was time to start my life, work and save money...but what the fuck did I want to do with my life? Logically, nursing or any other medical field made sense. There was always a high demand for it, but was it something I really wanted to do? This was going to be a pain in the ass. Couldn't I just read books and write for a living? Many cheers for the future of the unknown.

"We accept the love we think we deserve."

Stephen Chbosky; *The Perks of Being a Wallflower*

CHAPTER 7:
The Beast Within (Part 2)

Another day dawned. Sighing, I stared at the beast. The beast that stood over me, with an evil grin. I couldn't help but feel frozen, not wanting to deal with life, with the beast, always gnawing at me. Constantly going through life, surrounded by people unfamiliar with or lacking the knowledge to reason for my distance. Feeling out of place and insignificant in a familiar world. Regardless of the bright new day shining on through. Each day was either fixed and tiresome from the last attack or a continuation of the inner beatings.

Self-harm in many ways is an addiction of habit. Many people that suffer from symptoms of anxiety and depression find relief in such things. There are more options of self-harm than cutting. Oftentimes, people think of self-harm as simply cutting —because that seems to be what the media focuses on. Other means of self-harm include: picking, scratching, biting nails significantly, etc. Self-harm is put into two categories: intentional and/or unintentional. Intentional in itself involves deliberate harm on purpose.

When people self-harm by cutting, burning, and more, they are intentionally harming themselves. That mindset of wanting a release from the pain, a distraction, or even a simple reminder that they are indeed alive. I fell into that category throughout high school and part of my college years. Unintentional self-harm follows the end result of the "seemingly harmless" action.

During high school and the first two years of college, I intentionally harmed myself—I wanted to feel something, and be distracted from the emotional pain. It was an endearing relaxation for myself, an escape from reality. Some, including myself, find relief picking, scratching or fidgeting the items they have on them. Like wearing a ring and spinning it when you're anxious until your skin breaks loose over time. The best way to describe such an urge is a nasty mosquito bite. Do we logically know we shouldn't be twisting our ring around our finger until the skin breaks loose? Yes, of course. Do we know it's bad for us and we shouldn't be burning ourselves bit by bit to release an escape from our own heads? Again, of course.

We can remind ourselves over and over again of such things. Just like a mosquito bite however, the urge to scratch and give in to the temptation is ever so real. We know the facts of "The itch will be worse. The temptation will be greater." But the truth is we are creatures of habit. Which is one more reason why it is so important to find other ways to distract the mind when we are feeling so incredibly on edge. I am learning to force myself to write, color or even doodle when I feel anxious to try and distract my mind. Have the urges come back? Yes. They have for many people. You are not a failure for scratching that harmful mosquito bite. Taking each day at a time, breathing, and finding out your own strategies with dealing with mental struggles is one of the most important things you can do.

"If you don't think your anxiety, depression, sadness and stress impact your physical health, think again. All of these emotions trigger chemical reactions in your body, which can lead to inflammation and a weakened immune system. Learn how to cope, sweet friend. There will always be dark days."

Kris Carr

CHAPTER 8:
Well, This Is A Tough One

The week after I graduated high school, I went right away to my local community college to sign up for classes. During this trip, I also went to grab my first job. I knew I did not want to be a server; I didn't think I could handle the stress. I mean, who wants to be verbally abused every day over food? I mean, I get it; I love food as much as the next person—but someone can wait an extra minute or two, and the world will not come to an end. Thank you to those that work in customer service; I know many people can be grumpy when they're hungry.

In the end, a doggy day camp was the perfect spot to gain experience working with people and to play with crazy dogs. I spent several hours stuck in one room with no human interaction. Playing with puppies is like throwing someone in with a bunch of toddlers. As much as I loved animals, you soon find out who the pain-in-the-ass child is in the room. The cocker spaniel that came in every Tuesday and Thursday was a considerable humper— though adorable with all of its fluffy curls. But also a huge humper that would hump anything that moved. But if anyone else tried to hump him—I mean the other dogs, not humans—he would turn around and look offended.

Also, yes, some dogs will still hump even after they are fixed. After a few months, while waiting for my fall classes to begin, I spoke with one of my coworkers, Jim, who was leaving for a bartending job. We exchanged numbers, and out of the blue, the next day, he asked if I needed a roommate. He lived a few minutes away from the community college, I was going to attend. He and his female friend were looking for a third roommate to stay with them. It would be convenient, less than five miles away from college versus twenty. It made sense; I could still be close to my parents while gaining independence. That was part of being an adult. What was the worst that could happen? I went home and talked to my parents about moving in with someone from work—no worries; they had another roommate who was a girl. Nothing would happen, except that they understood I would keep to myself in my bedroom, study, and that I would not get involved with any parties. My would-be roommates casually mentioned that they were not into parties anyway and occasionally drank alcohol only once a month.

I ended up moving in within two weeks, hanging out with my parents once a week, and focusing the rest of my time on studying. Well, not all my time. The occasional drinking of alcohol was more like every day. The "they do not party" was also a lie. Surprise! They were both in their early 20's and very social. I was okay with them inviting people over. But every night was a battle having to go straight to my room and prop a chair against the door. Otherwise, someone would try to unlock the door and drag me out to socialize and party. Every day there was constant noise; I hardly got any sleep before my classes. One of my classes was at 7:30am. I wanted to show myself that I could handle any situation; I did not want to put my roommates in a lousy spot by moving out. They needed an extra hand to help. I just needed to work things out, find a way to adapt. I would try to socialize, so they would respect my decision to want to be alone sometimes.

Note to readers: dragging your socially anxious friend into a crowd is NOT a good idea.

Regardless, I discovered drinking relaxed my anxiety with the crowds. I forced myself to interact a bit, then go back into my bedroom to study and unwind. The first few weeks of living with my roommates, I ignored them and kept to myself. Soon though, I wanted to balance things, perhaps try to socialize a bit. Especially once I discovered that drinking helped calm my nerves. *Trigger Warning*

One Saturday night, I had a glass of wine and was talking with a boy about movies. He decided to go out for a smoke, and I followed along to keep the conversation going. I did enjoy talking with him at the time; he was kind, sweet, and didn't speak at all forcefully or loudly among the crowd. We went outside, and I kept him company during his smoke. Once he was done, we decided to walk to the nearby park—just this guy and I underneath the bright stars.

60

I couldn't tell you what came over me, but near the park I decided to lay down and stare at the stars as we spoke. The guy got on top of me and held me down, kissing my neck.

I froze; I kept telling him "No" and "Get off," but there was no movement or changes on his end.

Suddenly Jim's voice, which I never thought I would feel so happy to hear, called out from outside the apartment. "Aimee, where are you at?" Suddenly the guy jolted up and headed fast ahead of me towards Jim. I have no idea what he told Jim, but he ended up grabbing his car keys and leaving. I was quiet, confused, and went straight to my bedroom—locked it, and pulled my chair against the door. I didn't want to discuss anything; all I wanted to do was curl up in a ball and pretend none of it had happened.

A few weeks went by without incident. The parties continued, but my roommates seemed to have given me space and weren't trying to drag me out anymore. I was falling behind in my classes as I fell more into depression and trying to stay alive. My mind played tricks on me... 'You deserved it, you were naive and trusted someone you didn't know.' I pushed it into the back of my mind and pretended nothing happened. I spent a few months hiding my deep sadness, and told my parents nothing. I felt as if I was hanging on by a thread, being careful even with my breathing as I felt I might break. I was having more and more nights of crying in my sleep or crying on the way to school. I have always been an emotional person, ever since high school I became more aware of it. Though, when I became aware of it, I would tuck into a box and throw it in the closet, hoping to never open it again. I just have to keep moving, just have to keep a smile up—fake it 'til I make it.

One night, a rare party free day, Alexis watched a movie, and I joined her. We drank and ended up falling asleep in her and Jim's bedroom. We both heard a loud bang, what sounded like a bottle being tossed into the sink. Jim was angry about something again from work. He walked into the bedroom and looked at Alexis and me.

He started yelling at Alexis for various things. I wish I stood up for her back then, but I was scared of confrontation He started yelling at her and demanded that Alexis and I kiss since we had fallen asleep in the same bed. They weren't together; they were friends with benefits at most, but it was none of my business.

I refused, and Alexis whispered, "He's not going to let this go unless we do."

I kissed Alexis and got out of bed. Without going into further detail, he threatened and pushed me to stay. Honestly, one of my biggest triggers with my anxiety is being yelled at. His voice attempted to be calm at first, but then went into the stages of yelling. He threatened Alexis again. I remember looking at her, and wanting us to both leave. However, she refused to leave, and I finally found my footing and walked away. Jim did not follow me, nor did I hear anything else from their room. I walked into the room, and curled up feeling more vulnerable than I ever felt in my life. I should have screamed, I should have fought back. Instead, I froze, while I allowed Jim to touch me. While murmuring "No, that's enough." The next day I tried to convince Alexis that we needed to go. Alexis thought he was the only one who could ever love her, which was how things needed to be. I waited till they were out of the house. I packed up my belongings, left two months' worth of rent, and left. Alexis and Jim had history together, growing up as kids—they saw each other's horrors and thought they were each other's only hope of finding any kind of comfort. I needed to get out; I couldn't do this to myself anymore. I needed to escape when I had a chance.

I wish I could say that it was over. Jim's friends would text me for several weeks, calling me a "whore from the park," "innocently disgusting," and so forth. One of my friends from my neighborhood even said, "Oh, the apartment made you an adult" despite what I told her. I stopped speaking with her. I could not understand how she thought, 'Hey at least you gained life experience by being sexually assaulted.' I know at times, I do not know what else to say, but I at least try. It was not like I gained a unicorn from such life experience. Even then, I do not believe anyone would say even a dragon was worth it.

As human beings, we feel we will react in a certain way no matter what happens. Looking back, I wish I kicked and screamed or, better yet, left the apartment altogether at the very beginning. It wasn't my fault, though. It has taken me years to heal from that side of me. I was already a scared and unsure individual.

The events that happened at the apartment were not my fault. Many individuals who have been subject to sexual harassment or rape often feel the need to blame someone, and that someone is usually themselves instead of the person who rightly deserves the blame. Healing takes time, and while my parents did not understand why, I moved back home. I ended up seeing a counselor years down the road, and it was one of many topics that came up. I just wish I did it a lot sooner. I felt so much shame that I didn't fight back, that I thought I couldn't. However, with counseling, I have been able to understand and forgive myself for my own body and mind's reaction to the incident. I have moved on from it, but this chapter was still personally challenging for me to type out—I didn't want to go into any triggering details. However, I wanted to share this message with you: YOU ARE NOT ALONE. Every day is a continuous, healing battle. Regardless of the trauma that has occurred, it does not define you.

Yes, you hold ownership of handling your experiences, your emotions, and just trying to do the best you can in this world. Those statements about yourself and others can be filled with much judgment, such as "you should have..." "you could have..." and the most frustrating statement for events like these: "Everything happens for a reason." Those statements are okay if you ran a red light and were pulled over by a cop. Even if you flipped off that cop for giving you that ticket. Many can argue, "you should have been paying attention..." or "things happen for a reason and maybe pulling you over stopped you from hitting a llama crossing the road."

But with life, there are experiences that involve abuse, sexual assault, rape, and more. That simple casual statement of "things happen for a reason" doesn't work. And attempting to brush it off and seem like a wise old soul is bullshit. Life happens, but it's okay to not be okay about what happened. Not everything has to have a correctly set up plan of coordinates for this big plan called life. Some things go unanswered. I will never be able to answer A, B, C, or D for the multiple-choice question: "Why?" Things don't always happen for a reason, and our responses to those things are sometimes unplanned.

CHAPTER 9:
What Was I Thinking?

You know how there are those people who need to feel they have control over everything? I ended up being one of those people. After what happened at the apartment, I moved back home and stayed silent. I never told my parents what happened — only that I needed to be home. I was beginning to feel selfish for leaving my dad alone while he sat in the dark with his demons of depression. Any time I told my dad I wanted him to get help, it was always ignored — even the days where he fell asleep at the kitchen table. I would wrap a blanket around him and sit there with him, so he knew he wasn't alone. No one wanted to admit that my dad was going through something bigger than himself. I knew what that depression felt like, and I continue to feel and battle with it. I couldn't force him to get help; my mom would just wipe it under the rug, saying, "he's fine," because he never had any warning signs other than feeling depressed, anxious, and irritated at the world. I wanted to help, but... there was nothing I could do. I couldn't exactly become a bodybuilder, throw my dad in a trunk and drop him off at a psychologist. He had to realize that he needed help on his own, and I think that was the hardest thing for me.

My brother had moved out the year before. He moved to a different state, met a girl, and got married. So the responsibility was all mine to try and convince my dad that something was wrong. He would get bouts of anger anytime I asked if he needed me to help. While he was a stay-at-home dad, he perceived any efforts I made to clean or help him out as him being a failure. It was a constant battle every day, of wanting to help and yet getting into arguments with him.

His irritation and paranoid thoughts were becoming: "You don't love me. I could be a better father, and you don't love me. You want me out just like everyone does."

I couldn't help him; I felt utterly useless. I talked to my mom, and well, denial is a powerful thing when it comes to my family. After classes, I would make my way upstairs. I had looked up places where we could volunteer at, together, to get him out of the house. To help find motivation for him, but it wasn't easy. I tried looking up local events we could go to together; he always turned it down. Movie nights were out of the question. After a while, it became more obvious that I was walking on eggshells. The most random thing would irritate him and set him off. I was closing the microwave door too loudly. Or going into the kitchen when he and my mom were talking—he wanted to focus on one thing at a time. I shut myself out from the world, and spent less and less time talking on the phone, even with Lisa.

Lisa was always my partner in crime when it came to battling such thoughts. We had spent hours on the phone together, talking about whatever came to mind. Different breeds of dogs, wrestling-even though I was not into it. She met a boy in high school, and I am not sure what exactly happened but we began to drift away when we hit college. Perhaps, at some point I talked to her less and less with what was going on in my mind. There was no dramatic fight, or an event that pointed to the breaking point. We simply drifted away, day by day as we ran out of things to talk about. Day by day, as we shut each other out from our respective worlds. I attempted to ask how her and her boyfriend were doing. I do not think she wanted to go into too much depth. The last thing I wanted to talk about with her was what happened at the apartment. So there were gaps and missing parts that we each did not want to talk about. I think we each sensed that, and simply wrote it off as being too busy for the other person. It should have never been assumed, but that is often the reality when it comes from transitioning from high school to college. We no longer saw each other daily, and it felt like we had to have a reason to talk to each other.

I tuned out the world and jumped on social media. It was a few months after the whole apartment scenario. I was depressed and felt like in my version of normal there were moments where I felt hyper. On social media, I thought I could take on the world and then some, even with my anxiety with people. I wanted to escape; that was when I started chatting with someone online. There was an app on Facebook called "Hot or not?" How trivial, right? But it was also a way to meet new people and perhaps try at life again. After what happened, I was sure I did not want anyone touching me anytime soon. I don't know what I was thinking or why it was so unlike me. I was feeling adventurous and out of sorts. I met a guy online. We were smart about it; we met at a mall—and hit it off. We spoke about our interests, and he was very outspoken. Perhaps a quality that I was very much jealous of. He was himself, and with the many conversations we had together, he would have moments of anger and depression issues where he would fall off the face of the earth for days a time. He was stuck in his depression, and I would text him and call him, letting him know I was there for him.

Perhaps if I showed him that someone was there and cared, then he would care about living. I did not know it at first, but after a few months of dating, I realized he had spent 16-20 hours a day playing video games. I, for one, love games. However, he did not drive, nor did he have any goals for his life. I wanted to be there for him, to help heal his wounds. Yes, another one of those guys I seem to keep attracting. It was innocent enough. We would hang out once a week when I wasn't studying or at work. I tried to balance and see him for at least an hour or two each week, since I worked full time and went to school full time. Before I knew it, I was revolving any free time I had around him. Just out of work after being in my classes all day, I would drive over to see him and drive him to his friend's house—

so we could hang out. I would carry my backpack everywhere with me: that way he could be playing and spending time with friends while I studied. I thought nothing of it, at the time.

One day, a new video game came out. I told him we could try to get the game for him, if I had any extra money. I didn't mind, it was around his birthday anyway. But, my paycheck was a little low that one week. I told him I could not get him the $60 game, and I could do a $30 gift if possible. He yelled, screamed in my car and had a tantrum. He told me I was lying to him, that I just wanted to keep the money for myself. That I was ruining his life because his online friends were expecting him to be online tonight. I froze...and was confused about why he was getting so angry about something like this. He did not work; I provided everything if he needed help. I paid for everything if we went out. He didn't even try to find a job. When I suggested helping work on his resume—he would scream. This was not the man that I dated in the beginning. We had been together for almost a year. Honestly, it was the same guy—I just refused to see the hints of anger he would have when anyone told him "no." He pounded his fists into my car, and, when I broke up with him a week later, I told him no again.

I decided that this was not the life that I wanted for myself, and I was sick of him always yelling and screaming at me over nothing. He had no motivation to take care of himself, which I had offered to help him with, saying that I would pay for counseling. He wouldn't take any help from me, nor make any changes to himself. He would sometimes complain about not having a job, but then in turn say he was too good for retail or too good for any "below him jobs." A few days after breaking up with him, he called me to let me know that he was thinking about killing himself. I dropped everything and drove over to his mom's place, and no one was home except for him. He got into my car, clenching onto two notes—one with ideas of how he would do it and the other the note he would leave behind. I ended up taking him back over to my place, well... my parents' house. I could not help this aching part of me feeling responsible for his happiness. On the other hand, I also wanted to stand my ground this time, knowing I was not responsible for his happiness. I would try as much as possible to get him help, to force myself to hold him—it took me awhile to be okay with hugging him after so much happened in my life.

My parents didn't care who I had over, or at what time, so he ended up sleeping in the guest bedroom, and I fell asleep on the chair in the room. That very morning, I told my parents that Owen would stay here until his sister could pick him up—ideally, if she called back in the morning at least. Owen was going to play a video game in the room until I got back. I worked only for a few hours and returned to a surprise. The guest bedroom suddenly had my parents' dresser and a new set of sheets on the bed. Owen told my mother that he had nowhere to go. My mother had been so busy with working that I had forgotten to tell her I broke up with him a few days prior. My dad tried to tell her and update her, that we shouldn't just move him in without talking about it with me first. I know my parents are way too trusting; I love them.

Owen pulled me aside and showed me some job applications he had been submitting. He said he wanted to try harder for himself and for us. That he wanted to be a better man for him and me. That he would try his best to keep his anger in check and do his best to get better. I fell for it. I told him that I had dealt with depression in the past before; however, I would not stand around and be treated like a doormat.

Living with him was the worst thing ever. At first, it was okay. He would ask me how my day was at work, how my classes were going, and generally be interested in what I was learning. However, it soon got worse. He controlled when I saw my friends (if I saw them at all). He would guilt trip me if I ever left the house because he didn't want to be alone. Or sink into his depression if he was by himself. One day, he got angry at me because I went straight to studying instead of asking how his day was regarding his game. He got mad at me, started pulling his hair. I had to calm him down and even apologize for triggering his anger. It was my fault; I didn't greet him right away — he didn't feel like I loved him. It was my fault. I was not enough to make him happy. I confused my feelings of caring for someone for love. I loved Owen at one point; I felt I did. However, little by little, I thought I was drowning and worried about every little thing I did: would it piss him off? Because it was my fault, it always was, right?

CHAPTER 10:
The Beast That Breathes: Part 3

There are times where the lies of thoughts hold heavy, and are masked as truth. These times can be overwhelming and you can feel emotionally damaged by the links of memories that life holds. Regardless of logical thoughts, the monster still drips blood upon the soul. Depressive and anxious thoughts leave a foul stench. Never allowing a breath of calmness. Fear of judgement and tainting those around in the present day. Overthinking seems more and more like a common daily ritual.

The beast can come up with various names and be accompanied by its own allies.

There are times where depression and anxiety unite for a big powerful attack on the soul and destroy our view of purpose. The monster lies, but our minds continue to listen. Not because those that hold a monster do not try. No, that is furthest from the truth. The truth is that we exhaust ourselves with talking ourselves out of doing things. Sometimes, we feel the need to attempt to sleep the thoughts away. Please do not judge us based on the monsters we hold. Many will not understand and may even criticize our need for self-recovery. Those that recognize the monster go through the trial and error of trying to seal off the beast. All while working with the wizards that teach us spells and give us medication to help weaken it. But the beast learns quickly. As you level up, so does the beast. As you learn new spell combos, the beast learns how to defeat them. Thus, life becomes a continuous cycle of frustration and learning new spells and medications. Each day is different with its trials and frustrations—we never know whether or not we will wake up feeling okay or as if we will crumble from the weight of the world.

"Depression is so exhausting - it takes up so much of your time and energy—and silence about it, it really does make the depression worse."

Andrew Solomon

CHAPTER 11:
What Was I Thinking? Part II

Love and hate are, more often than not, on the same spectrum in some ways. Both push in heated moments and utterly blindside you, making you ignore certain realities, like the cockroaches all over the house trying to get your attention that something is genuinely wrong. Some may be obvious to others, but in that moment of trying to keep everything "happy and perfect," things can frequently burn down, values can be destroyed, and you ultimately hurt in all spectrums of pain. But when you follow through with that "Aha!" moment of fireworks, you realize that ending a relationship after many countless bruises, cuts, and heartbreaks should not be seen as a defeat but a necessary next step.

A few months had passed since Owen moved in. College was a way to escape from my home life. To pretend my dad didn't have depression, pretend that my parents weren't arguing more, pretend that I didn't have a controlling dick of a boyfriend. Maybe things would have been different if I could control *his* dick; perhaps then I would have threatened to blow it off like he would risk my life when he was angry. Nevertheless, I unfortunately do not have the ability to blow up dicks into thousands of pieces. Although it would be a very useful skill for dealing with threatening assholes.

One of my escapes at college was talking with my English teacher that I had the semester before. I ended up seeing her in-between classes, and a few other students ended up sitting in. We had a little group of people and would talk about books, writing, relationships, etc. I was part of this weird flock of people that met up through a mutual teacher.

One day, after meeting with my lunch group. I got an invitation from Vince, to go over to his house because he wanted to introduce me to a Mercedes Lackey Series. He had a few other books that he wanted me to have. Vince was a very outspoken individual. He joined the military as soon as he graduated from high school and serve from 2006 to 2009 as a Military Police Officer. His military career ended unexpectedly due to a medical issue in his left shoulder. Specifically, he had to have three surgeries to fix a labrum tear. When he joined our little lunch group, he was finishing up his physical therapy.

Without much hesitation, I said yes without thinking about any precautions or pissing off Owen. After getting Vince's address, I realized he only lived fifteen minutes away from my parents' house. I rushed home and emptied out my backpack. Vince made it seem like I was going to be bringing home more than three books out of his collection. I snuck into my bedroom, careful not to wake Owen up. For once, I felt happy that he was gaming all the night before; most likely he would be asleep for another few hours. There was no chance of arguments—I would go to my friend's house, grab some books and be on my way.

So I went to his place, and we made our way to the basement. Vince asked if I wanted anything to drink. He had some wine and rambled off a few other things. Then he said he could make me a raspberry martini — anything with raspberry, strawberry, or... well, who am I kidding? I love fruity anything, and it is one of my many weaknesses. I hardly had anything to eat that day. He poured the martini and poured himself one — I ended up drinking both.

We ended up talking about the *Obsidian Trilogy*, a series that he thought I would absolutely love. He handed me a few of the books and put them on the table. We got to talking some more, and he mentioned this show called *Dresden Files*. I was honestly super excited, I checked my phone to make sure Owen wasn't trying to call or text me. I told him if he was free, that I could watch an episode or two. So we plopped down on opposite sides of the couch and started watching *Dresden Files*. After the second episode, he excused himself to go to the bathroom and said I was more than welcome to help myself to anything. Well... I ended up trying to make myself a martini and put a bit too much of everything. Suddenly I went from "Wow I feel amazing" to seeing Vince spinning as he walked back into the room. Also, I kept complimenting his eyelashes—I mean, come on, how can one not be jealous of long girly eyelashes! Vince went upstairs to grab me some crackers and told me he would keep my keys until he knew I was safe to drive. I remember repeatedly apologizing for drinking three martinis. I lay down, trying to calm the spinning storm going through my head, when my phone rang. Just as Vince said, "Don't sit up too fast," I sat up like the world was ending and it depended on this one phone call.

It was Owen. "So I can't have a new video game and you're out and about grabbing books?"

I took a deep breath. Had his voice always been this painful?

"Owen, the books were free. I do not want to argue about a video game right now. I need to tell you something..."

I was about to tell him about the alcohol when he started talking more loudly.

"Well when are you bringing food? I can't believe you. I wake up, and I expect you to be here. Then, you aren't here. What am I supposed to eat? You were supposed to cook."

I paused for a second, tilting my head and wondering... did he always say stupid stuff like this? Wow, I'd been so blind to my situation.

"Owen, there is pizza in the freezer. I had a martini or two and am not feeling well."

Owen said, "I don't want to go downstairs and put a pizza in the oven. You're supposed to cook."

I placed my hand over my head, wishing for him to vanish so there would be no more noise. Vince went back upstairs to refill my water, as I finished the conversation with Owen.

"You okay? Do you want me to talk to Owen and let him know you're okay?" Vince offered.

I looked down at the floor, closing my eyes, knowing that any light right now was going to be the death of me. "No, no it's okay. I told him I would call him back in an hour to check in."

An Hour ticked by; Vince was reading a book and trying to be as quiet as possible while I closed my eyes and rested. Right on the hour, Owen called me only to tell me it had been an hour and I was not home yet; I told him once again I wasn't driving home intoxicated. He then told me I should walk home and that would wake me up. Right, because that's safe. I told him to give me another hour, to drink water and relax. He was pissed off, but the first time, I couldn't care less.

Later that night, I was ready to drive home. Vince packed me some crackers and a bottle of water if I didn't have any at my parents' place. Vince asked me to text him when I got home, so he knew I was okay. He apologized for not watching my drinking. That dork, I had three martinis in an hour. How was he supposed to know that I hardly drink and that I had nothing to eat? As soon as I walked in the door, Owen was downstairs sitting in the kitchen. He barely said anything. He stated he made pizza once he realized I wasn't coming home until about midnight. I could have one slice if I wanted. But the rest was his since he cooked it. I didn't grab any and went upstairs to pass back out onto my bed.

That morning a magical lightbulb came on regarding everything that happened the night before. I'll say evil and magical, because light and thinking are not a hangover's friends at all. Owen had no care in the world about my safety or the safety of others. All he cared about was what I provided and what he received out of it. Nothing happened that night with Vince and I. He sat on the other couch the whole time. Assisted me to the bathroom when I needed it. Grabbed me crackers and something to pack up to eat on the way home or at home if I needed. He sent me a text the next morning, apologizing again for getting me drunk. I need to remember to eat. I had known Vince at that point for almost a year through our lunch group. How natural it felt hanging out with him. Yes, the alcohol helped the wall break down—but how respectful was he. He actually cared about my well-being and asked me for my opinion. That had never happened before; anytime I talked to Owen or tried to about anything he would nod his head, half-listen, and if what I said angered him then he would let me know.

That same afternoon, I apologized to Owen for being drunk the night before. Yet, what slipped out of my mouth next, was something I did not plan on asking.

"I know you don't enjoy using the 'love' word a lot. But I was curious about why you love me."

"You're cute, you buy me things, and you tolerate me," he said, confidently, as though he gave the smartest answer ever in history class. He went back to the guest room to play his video games. I stood there, utterly frustrated with how little he thought of me.

I had stayed in the relationship and tried to give it my all, which had resulted in him being dependent, to say the very least. A few days had passed since that question. I had mostly kept to myself with books, studying and working with the pups at the doggy daycare.

After work one day, I approached Owen and said that we needed to talk. He rolled his eyes and said, "babe, I'll get better. I'll clean sometime this week or something." I blinked a few times, unsure what exactly to say next.

Not that his statement changed my mind, as if he had just presented a baby unicorn for me to keep. But the simple answer that he gave of "I'll get better" for a week and then expect me to do everything got to me. I had fallen for this hope every time, thinking I could somehow get him to want to change. Get him to care about life. Have something he wanted badly outside of himself that he wanted to fight for it. Somehow, I still wanted to be able to say that "love conquered all" by giving him everything he wanted and trying to motivate him to improve his life.

But, that wasn't right on my end either. If I was going to be with someone, I needed to accept and love them as they were. Someone I could continue to grow with, together and separately.

I was and continue to be a different person than when I first had feelings for Owen. I had always felt responsible and at fault if he wasn't happy or was angry towards me, and I felt it was my fault if he chose not to continue living. I stood there, taking in all my thoughts of the next action. And accepting this similar and yet different sense of self, even compared to a few months back. The words I wanted to say spilled out.

"Owen, I'm done with us."

His angry voice came out. He said, "Excuse me?"

I took a deep breath, as though it was my first time breathing. Seriously, thank you random unicorn light for showing me everything I had been missing.

With no hesitation, I told him, "I'm done being with you. I've done a lot of thinking. I had loved you for a while. Or perhaps at some point. I think I realize that love was misplaced, though. I wanted to love the person who I could see potential in. As silly as that sounds. I wanted to give and be a reason that you wanted to live and try harder. I can see that now, as that was my fault. You have way different values than I do. I kept trying to show you love. Show you I care about you and hope you could see that you are worth more than you think. You took my over caring self and used it to control me. I can't keep doing this."

He pushed the chair to the side and walked straight into my face. "If you leave me, I won't have anywhere to go. I may as well kill myself if that's the case. Maybe I'll do it right in front of you too. I'll write a note and make sure everyone knows it is your fault."

"Please pack up your things today. I'll call someone to pick you up. If you try anything, I will call the cops. I already called off work today to make sure you are out of here and not going to do anything."

It was just the two of us in the house. My father was at the gym, and my mother was still working at the nursing home. I ended up helping him pack because right when I left the room he went straight to his games. He kept repeatedly saying how he wished he could choke and kill me, then kill himself so everyone would think I had it coming, and he was the victim. I did not respond to his threats. The only care in my mind at that moment was him being gone and to be very careful over the next few weeks. I wanted to follow through with this, and the last thing I wanted to do was fall into his trap. Just as he was packing his stuff, one of my cats ran into the room. I heard him mumble, "I'll twist that cat's neck if he gets close to my game system." How in the world did I not notice how much of a toxic person he was? He seemed so patient and kind when we first met. I suppose some people are good at masking their anger and resentment, but only for so long...

I dropped him off that evening at his mother's house. I cried and hugged her. She had so much on her plate already and knew her son had anger issues. But she did not know the extent of them. I never entirely told her what happened, but I wished her the best and said that I would be there for her if she needed anything. The next day, I dropped off the rest of his stuff. A week later, he walked over to my parents' house while I was at work to talk. My dad called me and told me that Owen was over and he was refusing to let him inside. I rushed home and told my dad if I wasn't back inside in ten minutes to call the cops. He grabbed his phone and stood outside to make sure I was safe. No way was he giving me ten minutes alone with this guy. My dad had been working out more, and sometimes Owen would yell—but my dad thought he was yelling at his video game instead of at me. Plus, at the time, I told my dad nothing of what was going on.

Owen said he missed me and wished we would get back together. I will not lie; his words almost felt meaningful. I looked at him, unconvinced.

"No, you miss me because I'm cute, right? You miss me because I would buy your games. You miss me because I would tolerate your crap." Were those tears? He had tears in his eyes and he tried to wipe them away. Do not back down, I kept telling myself. I caught myself and almost offered to drive him home. He walked away; I looked back at him, making sure that he kept walking. After that, I told my parents everything that happened between Owen and I. They felt guilty. They didn't know what was going on under their own roof. Well, I didn't even know what was going on either. I didn't know how much damage I was causing myself from being with him.

CHAPTER 12:
Meet the Parents Cake

Once upon a time, in a faraway town. Well, not too far away from the city of Chicago, there was a girl who met a guy through a mutual teacher. With the oddness of fates, she, the guy, and a few other students would simultaneously visit the teacher. Thus the odd group was formed. Little did she know this guy would change her life. The guy soon became her friend and would talk about books and about history—one of the many topics he enjoyed talking about and discussing. One day, after a much-needed hangout introduced strength in her to shove her middle finger in Owen's face (her boyfriend at the time), she then trotted off with her fiery dragon and conquered the world.

All is true except for the last part. A dragon would be unique after many inner battles with discovering the love and care one deserves. Actually, things started feeling normal pretty quickly. I ended up hanging out with Vince every day. We ended up finishing up *Dresden Files*, one of my favorite shows of all time. And we discussed Mercedes Lackey's series *The Obsidian Trilogy*. After that, he suggested another book series called *Codex of Alera*. Little by little, this guy kept introducing me to new books. That is all a girl needs in her life: books, wine, animals, and a blanket. What else can anyone ask for?

A few weeks passed, and before I knew it we were holding hands on the couch while reading our books and merely being in each other's company. There was no declaration of "we are dating now!" Everything just seemed natural. Owen and I had been together for two years, so to the outside world I knew it seemed fast. But everything felt right with Vince.

Vince brought Owen up once. He asked, "what if Owen comes back and says he changed?"

I said, "If he changed, great for him. Too late now, though."

We left it like that. Humanity is strange; why do people like to be in groups again? After a while, I felt so responsible for Owen's well-being that I had mistaken it for love. I had "never give up on someone" engraved into my very soul. Although in the beginning of our relationship, Lisa and I weren't talking as much as we normally would. There were times we reached out to each other, perhaps once every few months, to see if we could hang out. Anytime we found a day that our schedule aligned, Owen would object. Then when I would offer to go by myself to hang out with Lisa and her boyfriend, he would get angry and emotional. I never told Lisa the real reason, but it seemed like I was becoming a flake. Letting Owen control me played into my emotions, making me feel that I was at fault if he was upset.

Once Owen and I broke up, I sent Lisa a long text explaining and apologizing over and over again for pushing her away. Lisa absolutely understood, and also apologized for us not being close and her not knowing what was going on. All in all, we started talking more like nothing had changed. As though we were back in high school, and our conversations were natural.

Once I started dating Vince, I told him about my friends Erik and Lisa whom I had pushed away during my previous relationship with Owen. And wanting to reconnect with them. He encouraged meeting them and getting back the friendship I once had with them. Lisa continues to be a sister to me, and Erik is my socially awkward brother that I have finally achieved hugging status with. I always understood Erik's Autism in a sense, even without him labeling himself with it. He would occasionally mention it, but I never thought of him as being any different. We both poked fun of each other's social awkwardness and the irking moments when people think it's okay to hug or touch each other on the shoulder at random.

Vince knew right away that I came with baggage. I did not tell him about the apartment event until much later in our relationship. But he knew from the very beginning that I apologized for everything, and it took me a long time to break that habit. I was talking too fast when I got very excited about a topic. Vince would never ignore me, even when I went from talking about books to randomly talking about what if the Grim

Reaper was a cat? He would listen and keep up with my routes of conversations. It was as though I secretly downloaded the "Aimee playbook and guide: How to understand Aimee's Awkward soul" and sent it over to him. I would love to have that playbook too. I cannot even keep up with the conversations I've had or the ones I expect to have. How dare people not follow their lines when I am talking with them? I'd be preparing for their response, and then they'd throw a curveball.

Vince was and continues to be one of a kind. He had a rough upbringing from birth. He was allergic to everything; his mom ended up having to make everything from scratch. However, Vince was the reason why his mom got into nutrition. Vince had all sorts of allergies, including the fact he died on the table with the first round of baby vaccines.

Side note: Parents, this is INCREDIBLY RARE. Sorry if I ended up putting another "What if?" in your mind.

However, because of the tough upbringing Vince had during childhood, he has the best relationship with his mom. They only had each other for years while living in poor conditions.

Vince's mom ended up getting a nutrition-based job and moved up within the company. Because of this, Vince is in tune with his emotions and with the individuals around him. Honestly, it's sometimes scary how in tune he can be. I would feel down, and he would know right away, even before I mentioned anything. He just knew the blueprint to my soul. Vince was different and way smarter than me. One of the first times I met Vince's mom, she said, "Vince was older than I was when he was born." because he has always been a responsible kid. On the days that his grandmother would watch him, they would watch the History channel together— before it was ALIENS! and cats riding unicorns in space.

When I told my mom about Vince, she decided I needed to marry him right now before I fell back into my pattern of dating men who I felt needed to be rescued. That, or perhaps she was worried I would scare Vince off with my awkwardness. I told her that he already knew that I was awkward. I mean, he already experienced what it was like taking me to a new place.

Walking into a new restaurant was nerve-wrecking. I told Vince that I needed to look up the menu to know what to order and expect. As we sat down, I looked to see if I could see the bathroom sign, exit sign, and anything else that I may want to monitor if my body panicked. I took a deep breath and reassured myself that everything was fine. The server came over; I smiled, knowing what my answers were to anything he could ask. I had my answers ready to go.

"Hello, would you like to try some of our wine? We have..." And then my mind blanked with the introduction of new information. I heard something that starts with a "C" and maybe an "R." I froze in place. Wait. I don't drink wine that often. Do I like red or white? What the heck is a Riesling? Why didn't I look at their wine menu? I knew I wanted wine, but why couldn't he just ask: red or white?

"Um... the one that started with an "R" please."

I already felt defeated by life at this point. Looking at Vince, I saw nothing but kindness and a bit of a smile. I swear this guy loves it when I am nervous. According to him, "it's cute," and it just shows him he needs to help calm me down. Jerk.

Vince gave me a few minutes to look over the menu; he always ordered the same pasta that this restaurant had. This was a big mistake, I already knew what I wanted, but now I was questioning what I wanted.

The server came back and asked if we were ready; I quickly said yes, even though I debated five other things. Where is my "R" alcohol? Right... the Riesling.

"I um... want this one?"

I pointed nervously on the page and had him look at what I had pointed at. I didn't even know what I pointed at, but he nodded his head and quickly said the name of the dish. I followed through with my choice of whatever the heck I was getting. Vince ordered his food, and I was beginning to get light-headed as I quickly grabbed my glass of Riesling and took a few sips.

"I didn't hear what he said. What did you order?"

"Vince...I do not have a clue what I ordered. As long as it's not Octopus eyeballs, I think I'm good. Guess it'll be a surprise."

"I hope you didn't get their beef tongue," Vince said, drinking his Dr. Pepper.

"Wait. Do they have beef tongue? No!" I panicked, he laughed a bit.

"No, they do not have beef tongue. Pretty sure you pointed at the pasta part of the menu. I suppose that's one way of trying something new, though. Just point at it and hope for the best."

We enjoyed the rest of the night with no instances, and the world did not explode in a fiery blast of zombie kittens.

"Pretend you are good at it." seems to be my daily quote.

My mom was not convinced by my story of one of my dinner dates with Vince.

"Well, how about I meet him. I can cook!"

I paused, almost choking on the water that I was drinking. My mom, as much as she is the best caregiver anyone can ask for, when she tries to cook, she gets distracted, and then something happens. She forgets if she put four ingredients in and then she improves. I secretly think that she loves making up recipes and hoping they work. She does not cook often, but our family never complained. I mean, we all agreed that my mom and I have sensitive stomachs—so an excuse to have tums and other over the counter stomach medication around.

"Oh, mom, you don't have to cook. I mean, I know you've been working a lot. How about we order in, and you can meet him that way?" I offered. When my mom had her mind on something, there was no arguing with her. So nicely suggesting something else was the only way around it.

"No, it'll be fine. I need to use up some vacation, and your birthday is coming up. He is off from work on Wednesdays and Thursdays. Invite him to dinner Thursday night. We will have food, talk, and I'll quiz him."

That was my cue to prep my boyfriend that he needed to move far, far away. The next day, I hung out with Vince after he got off work. We tried to squeeze in time to see each other as he worked nights. And I was still working full time and going to college full time (online).

"Vince... I have something to tell you," I said nervously.

"Is Owen back? Did he call you?" he said, concerned.

"What? No. My mom is off work for my birthday."

"That's great! I know you said she worked a lot," Vince said, as we sat on the couch at his house.

"Yeah, well... she wants to meet you. My dad wants to meet you too. But my mom is cooking."

"That's fine. I'm not picky with food. Especially when it's made by someone else. Never complain about food when someone else is cooking it."

"Yeah, I know. But...I can't cook. My mom tries, but..."

"It'll be fine. However, if she brings up Owen, you know I am going to say exactly what I think about the guy, right?"

"Yes. Yes. I know. But we should get some extra tums. Just in case, some ice cream in case the cake is bland. And I'm...trying to think about what else."

"Aimee, it's fine. I have an army stomach, remember? I was in the army for a few years before going to college. I can eat anything."

"Okay... but... um... don't say I didn't warn you."

A few days later, my boyfriend met me at my parents' house. I took a deep breath and looked down at the bag of items that I had bought. Vince was going to bring the ice cream. Just as Vince and I entered the kitchen. My mom walked quickly at him, hugging him in place. My mom pulled him away and asked him a bunch of questions. From where I was, I could only make out

Vince replying with, "Um... did Owen pass any of these questions?" I am guessing my mom was asking if Vince worked and if he had a car. I got the plates out and ready and told my dad to come downstairs, guessing mom shooed him away from the kitchen.

We took our seats, and everything seemed to be going fine. Just as I heard the oven beep, I looked at Vince and whispered, "remember. I got supplies." Just then, my mom walked in with the cake wiggling. Yes, the cake was alive!

My description of the cake: It jiggled and had splattered yogurt on top. Also, it was white with flour on all the edges of the cake. It was a jiggling chocolate jello that was pretending to be a cake.

Vince's description of the cake: Moist (sorry for the wording) and the driest part was the bottom. Also, the yogurt on top looked like strawberry splattered jizz. Oh! And, there was a full egg in the middle of the cake. Guessing Aimee's mom forgot to mix it thoroughly? Kind of impressive that there was a whole boiled egg in the cake. Perhaps cake art?

Needless to say, after the cake Vince realized I was not just anxious for nothing. I was worried about his stomach handling anything that was cooked in the household. I swear if there was ever such thing as multiple gods, the food gods have cursed our family with not being able to cook. My parents ate the cake, the whole "don't waste food" aspect. We both said we were full and went upstairs to my room. We searched through my purse as though we needed to find a $100 bill looking for medicines. His army stomach did not agree to the cake.

I suppose lessons were learned...

1) Trust the odd girlfriend with the odd family

2) He stayed even with the stomach cramps of death. Maybe they felt like period cramps to him. Regardless, now he knows.

3) He still thanked my parents for having him over and cooking. At the same time, his army stomach was screaming and perhaps swearing at him.

CHAPTER 13:
Nursing Home Edition

After working at the doggy daycare center for a few years, I tried out a different job. I was on my last year and a half with college. When I first went to the community college, I did not do so well on the entrance exams. So, I was put two levels lower for math and English—which also put me two semesters behind because I needed to pass the lower level classes before I could take the "regular classes." Thank goodness for low test scores, though! I wouldn't have met Vince otherwise, or the group of people in the little lunch group we formed.

My new full-time job had me working nights at a nursing home, as a caregiver. There were three floors of the building and over 70 residents. Most of the residents that we had in our care were declining and experiencing Alzheimer's. For those who may not know exactly what Alzheimer's involves, it's a draining disease that causes distortion in the users' memories, specifically in regards to time. Thus, memories overlap, and regardless of what others say to them, the individual in question is experiencing their truth. Their truth could be that their husband just left for work and wasn't home yet, even though their husband died ten years previously. One option is telling the person that their husband died over ten years ago. Their world crashes in front of them; they get confused, angry and may say, "No, I just saw him leave." Or, you can calm the person down, and say, "Your husband must be running late. I can make you some tea?" Because in all reality, they will forget that you told them that their husband died, but will remember the pain that was brought up again.

We had one lady named Mary. Mary could be the sweetest person ever or the most pissed off person in the morning. She would wake up screaming about her husband not being home yet. It was never a good idea to tell her that her husband had died ten years ago. The times where she was angry I would listen to what she had to say and what she was stressing about. I nodded in understanding, listening to everything she was saying. I sat down next to her if she allowed it.

"Mary, does your husband sometimes work late. Later than normal?"

She would nod, confirming that her husband sometimes was forced to work a sixteen-hour shift.

"Your husband may have forgotten to call you or wasn't able to. How about I make you some coffee? I'll check up on you." I would go downstairs, make her a quick cup of coffee and come upstairs and hand her the cup. Then she would typically swear at her husband for not calling or call me her daughter's name. We would often laugh at that; some men do not know how worried we get about them.

Then she would call her husband a "chicken fucker." To this day I'm not sure why she would say that, but I was not about to ask what a "chicken fucker" was. One of the many mysteries of the world that I decided I was not curious enough about.

Mary was my gal, regardless of the mornings when she would be angry, not knowing where she was. She'd curse up a storm and hope I would go die somewhere. She often would get aggressive and threatful for a few minutes. Most of the time it deescalated as long as I kept talking to her calmly. There were times though where nothing I said worked, so I would step out for a few minutes and then come back in and try again. At that point, I might have become someone else that she wanted to talk with.

One of my other residents throughout the nightshift was miss Ellie. Ellie was someone that would say the darndest things. Even when she was angry, she sounded more like a pissed off kitten that wouldn't stop meowing and trying to show how serious she was. There were nights where I would change her in bed, and she would say things like, "The bats are watching you!" And "my heart wants tea." However, one particular night gave me goosebumps. Ellie had a habit of waking up at 2am, walking around naked, and going door to door to the other resident's rooms to ask for "biscuits and tea." No matter how angry someone got at her for waking them up, she would keep on smiling and refer to them as her friend.

One night wasn't remarkably different. I would make my rounds every thirty minutes and would catch her most of the time before she wandered off on her quest of thirst and treats (we had a resident on the second floor that I would need to be on close stand by with). At around the expected time, I saw her down the hallway butt ass naked. I grabbed her bathrobe and walked towards her to cover her up. She was never concerned about her full-on nakedness in the halls; at least she'd never said anything about it. I went through the same routine of offering to make her tea before bed. As we walked towards the kitchen, she said the following: "You are so young and beautiful." I couldn't help but smile at this little British lady. Then she said, "too bad you are going to die so young." Then, before I knew it, she'd returned to saying, "biscuits and tea," as if she didn't just say something that completely threw me off guard.

She said it in such a matter of fact way, akin to saying "I see dead people," and then completely changed the topic. She still got her tea and biscuits before bed. She smiled all the way as we walked into her bedroom so I could tuck her in. Perhaps she had some twisted humor that I never knew of, or... perhaps she really sees "The time of death." Sweet ol' Ellie that gave me the goosebumps that night ended up passing away in hospice a little over a year after that. My heart tore in different spots, but it was something that was expected. She was one of the sweetest people I'd ever, regardless of what she spoke about with that smile of hers.

One of the hardest things with working with individuals with Alzheimer's or having a loved one go through it is seeing what they used to love vanish before their eyes—like forgetting the name of their favorite dog, or not realizing they were once married but remembering they lost a loved one a short time ago. The different spots of personality that they relive, positively or negatively. One of my other residents, who I casually mentioned above, had this inkling for a few months straight to get up on her own throughout the night. We had to have someone stationed nearby and be ready when the sensitive bed alarm went off. Her heart was pure as gold. I have never seen her angry except at herself, and that hurt. She would get mad that she couldn't walk as fast. And I would ensure her that it only meant more time for us to be together as I helped her to the bathroom. Sometimes she got up so quickly, the bed alarm roaring through the hallways, and I'd run in there. She'd be standing up and announcing that she passed her nursing exam. I would always congratulate her, even on the days that she would get up in a panic, thinking she missed the exam. I would show her the time and she'd say, "that's too damn early to take a test. Why am I up?"

And I would take care of her and tuck her in bed. She was one of the ones that had the most significant influence on me, even if she may not have realized it. We had to change a few of the residents for breakfast before the morning shift. (Side note: Yes, we had to be the assholes to help get people up at 6am. Some weren't too happy about it). It was a quick mistake of placing her shoes onto her feet before even putting on her new pants. I apologized to her and said we had to back up a step. The second time I apologized, she simply said, "Sorry about this? Don't be. This little thing won't matter in years to come. So why worry about it?"

I wish it worked like that; logically what she told me made sense. However, worrying was one of the many things that happened with anxious minds. There are nights that we drift into sleep, when suddenly, our brain reminds us of the time that we may have come off rude to someone. Or the time you answered "Yes!" to a server's question of "Soup or Salad?"

Anxiety isn't always logical, nor is there ever a reason. Yes, some emotions are felt without a set reason. Surprise! Emotions haunt the very soul and resurface at the most random times.

During my years at the nursing home, I met some incredible people that fight every day with memories as if they were their present day reality. One individual was a nurse some years ago. There were times that she would get out of bed and start getting ready at two in the morning. Her bed alarm would go off, and I would bolt over to her room because she was a fall risk. I would walk into the room and see her getting dressed and she would say, "I can't sleep. I need to make sure

I am not late for my nursing exam." She was so excited and ready to go, despite the reality that everyone else was living in the moment. To her, the most important thing was getting to her test. Little did she know, she passed and was a nurse in the army for several years. She had several children that ended up becoming nurses, and one that decided to become a counselor. But in that moment, all that mattered to her was living through her dreams. I would tell her that it was two in the morning, which it really was. She would look at the time, look back at me and question why she was up so early. I would tell her, but she was so nervous about the exam. We both knew how stress plays on the mind. I told her I would grab her some tea and be sure she woke up on time for her exam. Every week it was like this; I got into her habits quickly as she moved in. Every day I would walk around the same time, making sure she was asleep. Knowing exactly around the time she would try to get up, and then being ready to offer her some tea so she could rest before the big test.

After almost two years working at the nursing home, I ended up graduating with my Bachelors in Psychology. My dream was to try and get to work at a college, but I noticed many college counseling jobs wanted recruiting experience. So I started applying to recruiter jobs. I received a call within two weeks from graduating and I accepted the opportunity.

The last night, I was training someone that was going to take my place. Take my place as the daughter, take my place as the tea maker, take my place as someone who listened to individuals talk about their fears and dreams as if they were young and have yet to live. My nurse resident was declining quickly. She was no longer getting out of bed, but instead would toss and turn. She was on and off hospice care, and all the while a nurse was on the clock checking in on her. I still wanted to check on her and introduce her to the new girl. Death waited, I felt, as long as it could. After our quick greeting and letting the hospice nurse know that Eleanor was not sleeping,

we made our way to her room again. She was sound asleep and not in pain. That was one of the many parts that hospice nurses focus on, making sure the passing of the resident is as peaceful as possible. Sometimes residents will be on and off of hospice when they are declining and get assigned to a hospice nurse. This was to ensure the resident was not going through pain, and to make sure the family had the right resources and more intensive care. Her breathing was delayed and labored, her skin was cold to the touch. The hospice nurse had already told me; she did not expect her to live through the night. Just as I was going to go home for the day, I made my way upstairs. Something was telling me I needed to say goodbye, one last time with no one around. I made my way into her room. I was attempting to hold back tears. I had seen many pass away through working there. I had walked in on our resident's last breaths. However, hers was the toughest last breath I saw. I called the nurse right away, and she took her vitals—she was gone. Her soul was no longer in this plane. No longer would someone make her tea every night and ensure her that she would do great on the test. There is something about that sixth sense. Realizing the grim reaper was standing by. I remember whispering, "Good night, Eleanor; Peace be with you. "

CHAPTER 14:
The Odd Beginnings

Towards the end of working at the nursing home, Vince managed to buy his first place officially in November 2014. I was absolutely nervous about leaving my dad alone at home, while my mom worked her normal 60+ hrs a week. However, the place Vince picked out kept us within thirty minutes driving distance from them. And kept Vince about 45 minutes driving distance from his family.

The place he picked out was a beautiful 2-bedroom condo near the highway. Both of our parents helped out with the move and everything was going smoothly during the move and transition. We had situated our two cats into the condo. Indy, being the little adventurer he was, decided to run up and down the stairs, jump on every piece of furniture and claim the new place as his. Sylvester decided to sit in the corner for a day or two and take his time adjusting. Although Vince and I were dating for almost two years at this point, I was finishing up my Bachelors degree in Psychology. While it took me a few extra years to finish, due to having to take extra classes from testing on the entrance exam and taking some time off to save money, my degree would finally be completed by June 2015. I transferred my credits from the community college to a University about an hour away driving distance. The realization of not knowing what I wanted to do with my life dawned on me. Vince was working as a dispatcher over at a major hospital. His end goal was to become a security site manager once he got promoted to Assistant manager. My goal? I was working at a nursing home making less then $12 an hour. While it worked during the time I was finishing my degree, I knew I needed to find a career in my field. But where to even begin? With less than one year until I graduated, I had to start researching what jobs were available in my area.

Unfortunately, I knew for a fact that I would need to work with people. I wanted to help people in some way, whether it was through life guidance, career choices, resume writing, etc. But my anxiety had always stopped me from looking into anything new. I remember one night, while studying for one of my psychology classes, biting my lip and anticipating that I needed to prepare myself for something new. I couldn't just jump on a pretend dragon, fly away from all my worries and get a career in reading books. Though, if that was a career choice I would happily jump all over that. Then an idea that I had pushed away for a long time came into my mind. It wouldn't make the anxiety go away, but perhaps it was time I needed to look into medication. Help take the edge off so I did not feel the need to run away from almost any unknown situation. I do not have a problem do I? No way, I had been handling this just fine on my own for years. Then again, I'd been attempting to handle everything by avoiding anything new and then feeling the need to lock myself away from socialization. As Vince was getting ready for work that night, I looked up at him and casually asked him "How would you feel if I saw a doctor? Just my regular doctor and asked him about options for anxiety meds?" As he finished buttoning his shirt, he kissed me on the forehead. "If you feel you need it, that's fine. I just don't want you relying on the meds okay? If you want to try it out that's fine. Everything okay though?" I told him my concerns with needing to find a career, and the fact that I was already going through jobs and avoiding every single one in fear of the environment, the people, and, well...needing to talk to people.

A few days later, I made an appointment for my general doctor and discussed my anxiety. Without holding back, I had told him how I knew my anxiety was affecting me daily and that I wanted to make sure I got a hold of this before transitioning to a career. While I didn't know what career exactly, I knew for a fact that my anxiety was being a pain in the chest just thinking about something new, and that I felt light-headed anytime I believed I was going to do something wrong. The doctor suggested that I see a counselor with my meds, but I wiped it off. Yes, as a psychology major I knew that meds and seeing a therapist was always suggested. However, I didn't need that...right?

A few weeks into my new meds was, well...odd. The medication at first made me very sleepy and the doctor prescribed some emergency anxiety meds as well, in case I found myself in a new situation and felt a sense of panic. A few months passed, and we found more and more things in our condo that needed to be fixed. Although we had our place inspected before Vince bought it, our appliances decided that they did not like us. Things that could and would break indeed did within a few months. Our microwave was the first thing to randomly die. Now, microwaves in general are always finicky. They are either "Fuck that's hot! Now my tongue is a burn victim." Or generally some parts of the food are warm while the majority of it is cold. But it was at the point where it gave us neither option; it was simply dead. Then it came to our attention that we had a leak above the kitchen, directly underneath the guest bathroom. It would progressively get worse anytime someone used it. This meant I couldn't use the bathtub for a bubble bath during my monthly bloody battles, which resulted in me being a bit crankier during those times. We got everything fixed later, but it took time and of course a credit card for housing emergencies.

Six months in and we had to fix a lot of, well, everything. March came around, which meant lower car insurance for me. In the state of Illinois, when you hit the age of 25 your car insurance goes down. I had a few tickets on my record over the years, so a lower rate by a good $75 a month was going to be huge. I hit my 25th birthday, but unfortunately the lower bill lasted for only one bill cycle. Sadly, in the beginning of April my car was totaled...while parked. Did I mention I have bad luck? That morning, both Vince and I were looking forward to being off of work that night. I had just gotten home with a new set of pill casting spells to fight the anxiety monsters. We had decided to try new pills after a few months, due to the newly developed headaches I would get, and the meds started to upset my stomach at times. I parked my car on the street, as usual, because our lease only allowed for one of our cars to be in the parking lot.

Vince and I were prepping up to watch a movie while we waited for someone to come by and fix our air conditioner that had broken a few weeks back. As Vince was grabbing the movie snacks, he mentioned that while I was at the doctor's appointment he had taken out the trash and saw a couple screaming at each other outside the condo complex. Soon after, as the movie was starting, we heard screeching tires and a loud crash. Quickly, we stood up to look outside. What we witnessed was a white car that had crashed into a blue car and managed to push it two parking spots over into a work van. Vince said something along the lines of, "Well, that car is fucked up."

I nodded my head in sad agreement and said, "Baby, that's my car that's fucked up." Slightly panicked, I went upstairs to grab my information, as that was the only thing that I could think of to do. I always carry an extra copy of my car insurance in my purse, in case my car is too disorganized to find the main one. As I walked outside, the A/C repair guy showed up.

Vince stayed inside with the guy while I went outside to confront my poor car. Cops were already on the scene, and a cop was looking inside my car to make sure no one was in it. Without thinking, I said loudly, "Wow. My car got more action than I did this morning."

The cop looked up and slightly smiled and then went back to looking in my car. "I'm serious, that's my car."

When the cop still didn't seem to believe me, I said, "Why else would I claim a wrecked car?"

I gave him my information and got the details on what exactly went down. They received a call from a younger gentleman stating that his ex-girlfriend just stole his car. The cop turned into our backwards "C" shaped neighborhood and the lady in question was driving over 70MPH straight at him. The girl made a quick choice and instead of hitting a cop car head on, she decided to hit my small Honda Fit instead (thank goodness she didn't choose to hit the cop car!). The girl seemed physically okay, somehow. She was on the ground shouting, "Baby, please don't leave me!" over and over again while the guy stood back.

More people started coming outside and taking pictures of my murdered car, along with the other van that my car was pushed into.

I sighed and simply said, "Great, my car is one of those five minute fucked up celebrities."

I unlocked my car to grab all the jackets that I stole from Vince. Yes, significant others' clothing is always 100% better, more comfy and worth the steal. Soon after all the cars were taken away, I decided to give my dad a call to let him know what happened. My dad, probably not sure how to respond, asked me if I had my car taken in yet for an emissions test (Illinois vehicles are required to complete an emissions test every two years. Pretty much to ensure that you aren't driving a fucked up car). I laughed way harder than I probably needed to. I told him I would take it in, especially after the crash. But in all seriousness, thank goodness I delayed getting the new car sticker, the emissions test, etc. After I hung up with him, I called my mom right away and left her a message: "Mom, I am safe and okay. I am not hurt. Call me first before dad if you can." My dad is horrible at relaying messages. He would end up leaving my mom a message like, "Hey, our daughter got into a car accident and her car is totaled. Love you." Which would bring anyone into a severe panic. I ended up getting a new car, two weeks later, co-signed with Vince to help lower the payments. Thank goodness too for non-insured car insurance. Both the driver and the owner of the vehicle did not have insurance. Which meant his mom had to pay for everything. They were both minors in what seemed like a Lifetime drama type movie. After I bought the new car, my insurance went up because of everything that went down. Neither the guy nor the girl had their own vehicle insurance. My insurance had to pay for everything, and wrote me a

$4,000 check to get a new car. Back to making payments on a car, after I had just finished paying off my poor blue car.

About a month after the event, I had to go in to see the doctor again to review my medications and to notify him if they were working or not. I told him about what happened that first day I took the pills. I doubt they were in effect yet, but the fact that I was calm, collected, and sarcastic, was a huge win regardless. I felt overly calm about the whole situation, even days after the car event. Annoyed, yes, but anxious? Not so much. I cannot control life's oddities.

May 2015, almost two months after the car incident. Vince sent a picture to my phone of our shattered patio door. It was late afternoon at this point, and he was sleeping and getting prepared for a 16 hour overnight shift. When he heard a loud BANG! from outside. He put on his pajamas and went to investigate. He initially thought some kids were playing outside and threw a small rock at our glass patio. When he came downstairs, the first glass panel was shattered and barely holding on. I came home, and the cop was already there as Vince was filing a report with the police. We have no idea how or what had happened, other than a small hole in the bottom of the glass. It almost looked like someone shot a BB gun into our patio door. Our building association bugged us the next day to fix it ourselves and that it had to be a specific type of door and color (oh and they had no idea where we could get it from). So there was a bit of a delay regarding getting the actual door. After a week, we had cops coming to our place every day because someone called them and said our door was shot at and we were refusing to fix it. The association required that we get everything reviewed before adding or fixing anything, which alone can take up to 4 months. We finally had to tell the cops that someone was clearly harassing us as this was the fifth call in three days, even though the event had happened a week ago. We finally managed to get the door approved and fixed, which meant no more letters from the association saying we had to fix it, even though we had to wait on them. I also would like to note that we don't even live in a bad neighborhood. We just had a stroke of bad luck it seems in the first year of living on our own.

Toward the end of May 2015, I finally got my Bachelor's degree. At that time, my brother also graduated with his Masters degree in Theology from an online school. I never thought about walking for my Bachelors degree. The idea of dressing up, walking on stage to grab my degree, never got me excited. If I was able to, I would have skipped my high school graduation all together. I told my parents that I was not planning on walking on stage, and if they wanted to see my brother for his graduation that was completely fine by me. I had to work and was not able to take time off to go to my brother's graduation ceremony.

Now for the scary part, finding a career that I wanted to stick with for at least a few years. I knew for a fact I did not want to stay at the nursing home. I wanted to find something where I could help people and still be able to pay off my bills. I needed to develop new skills and find what I was searching for. I think nothing could have prepared me for talking on the phone. My end goal at the time was to become an Admissions Counselor for a college. I loved the idea of helping people take their steps to find the right career path. I loved the idea of creating a plan for people where they would set goals and assist them in reaching them. The ultimate enemy of my life? Phones. And well, talking to people I did not know. How could someone with social anxiety *want* to have a job where they helped people?

Being a counselor almost seemed counterintuitive. One of the essential things with social anxiety is the unknown factor. By becoming an admissions counselor, there is an opportunity to set up a work environment that can be controlled. Yes, I would talk to people, but there would be plenty of time to listen to their goals, stories, and what they wanted to achieve. I was naturally an overthinker and over-planner; I felt at the time that admissions counseling would be the best thing for me. I could help create a plan for people to follow and guide them through the process. I could encourage them to volunteer or work part time, at least, so they could build their resume and show off to the world what they were made of. I finished my Bachelor's degree and worked at a nursing home where I made just above minimum wage. Although I paid for most of my education by going to community college before enrolling in an affordable university, I had about $10,000 in student loans to pay off with interest. Thank you, Sally Mae (All the other student loans wouldn't accept me because my mom made too much money, even though I was the one paying for everything and working full-time). I knew for a fact I needed to find a career. Did I think about going to get my Master's? I did, but I knew for a fact I could not afford graduate school without taking more money out. I couldn't exactly go outside, wish upon a unicorn, and have it grant me three wishes for more money towards my education. I could have, but I doubt any magical unicorn would have come (without drugs utilized).

117

I knew I was deathly afraid of talking on the phone. I couldn't, but I knew I needed to try something. I started applying to jobs at random on Careerbuilder.com. This was going to be a test for me; I needed to get better and practice. Even if I felt like puking most of the way to any unknown social situation. Within a few days of applying to jobs, I received a phone call from a staffing company that handled engineering and aviation focused jobs. When I picked up the phone, right away, the manager began talking about the company. I froze on the spot and thought... did I apply to be a mechanic? I know nothing about tools? WHAT AM I GETTING MYSELF INTO!? Then, he casually mentioned that he used to bring his dog to the doggy day camp I worked at years back. I did not remember the dog... at all. But we talked about dogs for a good ten minutes. I can talk about dogs all day; I had to hold myself back from not writing about dogs at random in this book, so that you know.

I was brought in for the interview and got the job. Now here I am, in a position of talking to people...over the phone, for most of the day. What in the world did I get myself into? This job required me to go against every fiber of my being. Anxiety took over me, as I jumbled through words and made notes that I for sure messed up my interview. To my surprise, I received a call back the next day and a job offer. I put my two weeks in at the nursing home and began training to become a Recruiter for a staffing company. June 2015 marked my first month as a Recruiter, my first career right out of college.

Throughout the training, I was happy. I took down notes, color-coded everything regarding their system, rules of recruiting, tips, and so forth. That part I enjoyed, over and over again. I was able to stay quiet, listen, and organize my notes. I honestly would say one of the hardest things was faking being happy.

The problem with experiencing depression was the fact that all I wanted to do was shut down. The last thing I wanted was to pretend I was someone I wasn't—happy. The fear of being fired kept me pushing and trying to push down those depression days. Even though I smiled, I was barely holding my mask steady. Something was wrong with me; something was always wrong with me and I was not too fond of that part of myself. I was still so scared about saying the wrong thing, using the wrong item, pissing someone off. Something I was told in training worried me. I was told people would pick up on the phone if I was not confident. I am not a confident individual; I question myself daily, as the monsters take a ride in the back seat and begin yelling at me. In my previous job, I had the same fears—but not to this extent. This recruiting job involved people's lives. The voice in my head was telling me that I would never amount to anything, that maybe I was just not good enough for this job. Perhaps I wasn't even good enough to follow my dreams? All these thoughts came scrambling in.

Comparing myself to others had always been my monster's favorite thing to do. Logically I knew everyone started at a different point in their life. In my mind, though, everyone was a natural at talking to people. I always felt like I was a cockroach, crawling on the floor as everyone knew that I did not belong and just tolerated my existence. I called people constantly, left voicemails, picked up the calls that would come in. If I did not have a plan in mind, I scrambled. It was one of the reasons why I did not like answering the main line when people would call. I liked to be the one that called people; well, I got used to it at least. I can make notes on exactly what job I was calling them about and have a list of alternatives in case they did not want the particular job. This job was going to allow me to plan, organize and help individuals pave their way in their careers. All while I am trying to figure out how to not scare anyone away with my awkwardness. This was going to be a challenge.

CHAPTER 15:
Handling Your Armadillo Mode

As much as I wish that the moment I started dating Vince, my depression and anxiety went away, this was not the case. I realized that even if there was discovery of dragons and I could have one as a pet, my monster was going to be with me. I had packed it up, pushed myself to try harder and harder— without even realizing that my mask was breaking. After a few months of Vince and I dating, my days of depression hit out of nowhere. Too bad depression doesn't make a reservation. "Yes, can I have three days of depression please? With a bottle of wine and a jacuzzi? I'll be sure to clean up after myself." Depression symptoms weren't ever polite, nor did they provide much of a heads-up warning.

Vince and I were hanging out one night, when the sudden wave of emotions came over me. We were talking about a book, and I tried to keep up with our conversation. I tried, and I felt myself losing my grip and couldn't pay attention or hang onto his words. The emotions hit, and throughout the day everything became foggy. I kept telling Vince I just felt off. I didn't want him to worry, or feel it was his fault. But after a while, I thought about my own overthinking self. I would want someone to tell me the truth, otherwise my overthinking would take full control and I'd think otherwise. I pulled him aside; I was so nervous about how to put any of my feelings into words.

"Vince, I... I feel like curling up and crying."

Vince held me tight, and I told him that sometimes I got depressed at random. Sometimes it could be days, or perhaps a week. It could sometimes even come for a few hours like a tidal wave.

"I just want to curl up like an armadillo."

Simply telling him I wanted to roll up into Armadillo Mode seemed like the best comparison. He always curls me up with a blanket and my alpaca stuffed animal (Yes, I have one! No judgement. It's light blue, fuzzy and "Elpica," a made-up word from Epic+Alpaca) and lays down next to me. Vince is my biggest supporter, and the term armadillo has stuck within our relationship.

Throughout the years, instead of coming up with the words that I couldn't even form due to my mind feeling foggy, I would simply tell or text him "Armadillo Mode" so he was aware and knew why I was acting distant or wanted to be alone.

Armadillo Mode tends to range in intensity and yet numb emotions. Moments of overwhelming sadness that I feel as if I am barely breathing. Moments where my brain acknowledges that I am hungry, and yet I'm not motivated to eat. Those that struggle with Mental Health have their own way to react in their armadillo phase. Kind of like how there are different types of armadillos.

Armadillo Mode is not to be mistaken for the monster itself. But rather an emotional range of breeds when it comes to how our depression, anxiety, thoughts and so forth take over. My armadillo can range from my social anxiety, where I talk too much or too little, to wanting to curl up in a ball and attempt to sleep the anxious thoughts away. Or experiencing that mood where everything is numb, that my very existence feels irregular to say the least. Anxiety and depression at the same time is a constant pain in the mind, to put it lightly.

Do you know what it means when someone says they have weasels nipping at their very thoughts? Or feeling the need to curl up like an armadillo? To those that don't understand, I'm not saying that you won't. But know that those that fight the weasels, also fight the rabies. Along with the monsters. You see... the monsters are a part of us, and the weasels are an afterthought. They bite into our soul, while the monster laughs. Yes, we recognize the issue but the meds, the people, etc., don't make it go away. No, instead they build up our armor as in experience points in a game. Preparing ourselves and gaining knowledge on what works when the beast attacks.

There's more to the story than many let on, this is true. We find people, our tribe, that we can relate to. We acknowledge each other's pain. A tribe of flowers that encourages one another to grow and yet acknowledges the pain and the storms that life brings. When waves of depression and anxiety come for instance, it is not premeditated or planned. Rather it is a consistent battle of what is going on inside our minds.

The thoughts on how silly it must be to feel like this. Someone who does not know what it is like to experience such thoughts simply lacks understanding. There is no "on" and "off" switch to these thoughts. But I will tell you this, reader. You don't have to feel silly for the way you feel. If it's hard to describe your emotions and thoughts, simply saying, "Armadillo Mode" could help as a code word for those that you trust, especially when you don't feel like explaining such emotions, when you feel the armor start to go up and the need to fight yourself internally, just to get by.

There is no certain look that people with mental health issues share. It's how we take care of ourselves when we are feeling our worst. Even if it's just a little bit at a time. Please do not harm our armadillos by any misunderstanding. There are individuals that we absolutely love. Do not take offense when the armadillo shows up to protect and heal. Each one of us has our own battles that we need to face.

When someone is in Armadillo Mode/Depressed, it is best to remember to do the following:

1) Be supportive: Please do NOT tell them that they have no reason to be sad. Emotions should be

validated. It is one thing to not understand what they are going through. It is another to dismiss emotions.

2) Practice and Encourage Self-Care: Remind them and yourself that self-care is NOT selfish. If they need to recharge or attempt to refocus by tackling an art project to keep their mind off things, go for it!

3) Don't Take It Personally: Watching my dad being depressed was one of the hardest things in my life. I kept asking what I was doing wrong. What I can say is this: try your best to separate yourself from the cause. Take a deep breath, and do what you can in the moment. Do not however, blame yourself or feel that you are not enough. Depression can hit individuals that are famous. Depression can hit individuals that are rich and at the top of the world. Depression does not discriminate.

The emotions that many individuals go through, whether they're anxiety, depression, bipolar disorder, or something else entirely, burrow themselves deep inside and may never leave. Seeking counseling, medications, therapists and other approaches are not going to have a quick result. This means you have to prepare yourself for a relapse. I will personally admit, I have self-harmed before. Multiple times, and in multiple places throughout middle school and high school, as well as throughout my college years in a "not as bad" kind of way. It's been two years though, close to that at least, since the last time I did any harm to my body...on purpose, I should add (if we are counting clumsy times, then I'm at..."It's been four hours since I hurt myself. Carried a garbage bag to the dumpster, slipped backwards onto snow. Luckily dog poop was not nearby). When this happens, hopefully your support systems and coping mechanisms are close at hand.

There are going to be changes throughout life, as well as our responses to those changes. Medication adapting to your body is one of the most annoying things, because it may work for a while then your body is like, "I'm done with this cocktail. Let's have a blueberry, lemongrass one please." Then you have to go back to the therapist and wait for them to find the right ingredients and measurements. Oh, and finding counselors or psychologists that match you is a whole other matter.

Regardless, it's okay to not be okay. There's so much stigma against emotions other than happiness. Many people understand physical pain but may not be fully aware of emotional pain that comes from our memories, our circumstances or even from our very own brain. That doesn't mean you are a failure at the life that you've been given. It's a matter of trying to find a way to cope with multiple challenges. You, yourself are not a failure, but inside you there may be a core of experience that needs to be looked into. How do I deal with this depression beast this time? Step by step, breath by breath.

"I think the saddest people always try their hardest to make people happy because they know what it's like to feel absolutely worthless and they don't want anyone else to feel like that."

Robin Williams; Actor, Comedian

CHAPTER 16:
Mental Health Among Bloodlines

My grandfather on my dad's side passed away before I was born. From the stories I was told, he was loving and angry. My grandfather most likely battled PTSD and turned to alcohol to help shield the memories from the war. That much I gathered from a few of the stories that I have heard occasionally. But that is not my story to tell. A small-town community, everything was everyone's business. So mental health and seeking help was not something to do back then.

In my dad's adult life, he experienced points of depression and anger. My grandpa fell ill due to lung cancer in 1989. My brother was perhaps three years old. My dad's siblings were afraid of how my father would react to their father's health condition. Perhaps protecting the youngest sibling, they decided to keep quiet. My dad knew his father was not doing well, but he didn't know how bad it was. As a nurse, my mom found out from a friend (this was before HIPAA) that her father-in-law was dying. She confronted my aunts and uncles on why they wouldn't tell her husband. They said to her they were going to tell him after he passed. My uncles and Aunts had time to confront the grim reaper arriving soon, my father did not. He was notified days before the end seemed to be near. My mother had to be the one that told my dad that his father was dying from cancer and most likely wouldn't survive much longer. Knowing that my father and grandfather did not have the best relationship. My mom wanted to make sure my dad knew he had a choice to see his father on his deathbed or come to terms without seeing him again. My father saw my grandpa at the hospital to say his goodbyes. A few weeks prior, my mom found out she was pregnant with me. Just as my grandfather took his last few breaths, my father and mother told him they were expecting another child. My grandfather smiled, and a tear fell down his cheek. An hour after my parents saw him for the last time, is when my grandfather took his last breath. My father has many significant memories with his dad; there is no question about that. My grandfather fought many monsters of his own, that he had kept quiet about. Which, I suppose, affected many of the relationships he had in his life.

My father fell into depression's trap. He had a job working as a janitor for a hospital, but when he told the hospital that he needed to take off the next day because his dad was dying, the hospital showed him the door. Everyone expected my grandmother to fall into depression or perhaps no longer want to live. However, she ended up living 30 years without him. 30 years without constant anger. 30 years of continued silence, as she would never speak ill of her husband.

I could not say if my dad dealt with anxiety or depression throughout high school. I do not think my dad would ever tell a soul about it if he had. From my experience, though, he had depression and anxiety since I was very young, along with undertones of anger issues. He would yell a lot when he was at his breaking point. It was a constant daily rollercoaster. There were good days, where he would smile, hug, and we would be perfectly content doing nothing together. Then, there were times I would come home from school and notice he would be shut down on the couch, unmoving, and I would stand there, making sure he was breathing before heading to my room. I was just a kid; I may have thought he was sleeping, and I did not want to disturb him. Later I would find out that depression had been pushing him down for days, telling him lies of self-worth, that no one loved him, and that everyone was out to get him. Those thoughts ate him up at times, and he sometimes would lose the battle.

He would call my mom when he was anxious and paranoid six times a day at minimum to make sure she was at work. He would use us as his excuse for calling. "Our daughter and son want to talk with you." This led to fights when she would come home. Working sixteen hour shifts and continuously being paged that she had a phone call from her husband took a toll on her. His mind would keep saying that he had to talk to her every hour, on the hour, to make sure she wasn't dead. That something may have happened at work. Like a shooter, or she fell and hit her head. Well, the last one was likely, as clumsiness runs in the family.

My mother also had a history of mental health issues from growing up with her alcoholic and narcissistic mother. My grandmother on my mom's side would constantly say that we all hated her. I remember one day when I was around 5 or 6 years old and she took me to her barn to see the horses. I was absolutely terrified of horses. She grabbed my hand and forced me to pet the horse. I cried which scared the horse— the horse was probably like, "I am a majestic beauty why are you making noises?" But my Grandmother, like many times before, said "I hate you. You hate me so I hate you." She saw my fear of the horse as me hating her. I feared my mom's mother. Growing up and not being able to talk, she always belittled me. She would talk about how stupid I was in front of me because, since I couldn't talk, she thought I did not understand what she was saying. There are maybe a handful of okay memories of my grandmother. How every year she would make all of her grandchildren pajamas. I always got pink ones, even though I was not a fan of the color. However, I always appreciated the fact that someone could be so creative and make clothes. My cousins have glorious memories with my grandmother on my mom's side. While she was narcissistic towards them as well, she toned down her comments directly to the children. This was my truth, and my truth alone. My cousins can try to convince me that she was the best person ever. My truth was that, when I was with her, I was always called stupid for not talking. I would always be yelled at for not telling her what I wanted to snack on. My parents told her I had speech issues and we were working on it. She seemed to think that yelling me would magically make the words flow.

My mom's mom disliked the fact that my mom moved out of her small town. She hated that she married my father and decided that her two grandkids, my brother and I, were spoiled rotten for living close to the City of Chicago. That we clearly wanted nothing to do with family. That we hated her, all because of my parents' choice to move closer to the city for nursing jobs. Even though, anytime we saw her she would belittle us, especially me for never talking or looking up at her. When I was growing up, my mother was always at work and had always told us that she wanted to make sure that we had everything we wanted, unlike her own life growing up. When she was old enough to ride her bike and deliver newspapers in the neighborhood, she would often get her siblings gifts—because otherwise no one would have gifts underneath the Christmas tree.

In high school, while I never thought of killing myself, I did hurt myself. I hurt myself with burns in order to feel like I was alive after days of feeling so incredibly numb. Or I would burn myself if I made a mistake, so I could constantly be reminded.

I wasn't diagnosed with my cocktail of disorders until I was in the middle of my 20's. I experienced intense anxiety and depression, starting from when I was very young. Even when I saw a therapist for the first time, I downplayed my monsters and my emotions. I pretended I was someone else, who was confident and just dealing with general bullies.

After a few months of starting my new job as a Recruiter, I received a call as I was getting ready for work.

"Aimee, are you busy? Are you at work?" My mother asked nervously.

Hesitant, I replied, "I'm at home. Why?"

"Your father is missing, Aimee."

"Mom. What do you mean missing?" I sat up on my bed, as my heart skipped a beat.

"Your father never came home last night," she said.

"Wait. Where the heck did he go? He avoids people like the plague." I said, trying to make sense of the news.

"Your brother dropped him off at Walgreens to pick up his meds. I guess he told your brother that he would walk home, since your brother wanted to hang out with some friends while he was in the state."

Taking a deep breath, my mind trailed to the worst possibility... that he was dead. That he did something horrible to himself. That someone hit him and threw him in a ditch. My mind played games with millions of scenarios in the first minute of our conversation.

Interrupting my thoughts, my mom assured me that everything was going to be okay.

"Mom, I'll call off work. I'll say it is a family emergency. It's fine, I haven't called off yet. I hardly ever call off," I said, trying to stay calm as I wrapped my mind around everything going on.

"No, Aimee. I already spoke with the police. They said to go about everything as normal. I'll be home though just in case." How could she be so calm about this? Then again, she always had a calm demeanor.

"Nothing about this is normal," I mumbled, trying to stop my voice from cracking.

"Go to work, Aimee. I'll keep you posted. You better not start driving around looking for him."

Hanging up the phone, I held back my tears, unsure of what to do. I would be anxious no matter where I was. I called Vince to let him know what was going on, as he was already at work. I told him the same thing my mother had said. To go about our day as normal, and she will keep us posted.

I made myself go to work; I do not know how I got there. I know I drove into work, but it felt like I was on auto pilot. As I parked the car, I tried to call my dad again. His phone went straight to voicemail. I texted him, hoping that this was all some sick joke. I knew it wasn't, but my mind was coming up with a million different scenarios of what could have happened.

Throughout the day, in between phone calls, I was continually checking my phone. I was hoping for it to ring, but it never did. I texted under the table— keeping to myself and being quiet. I wanted this day to be over and to hug my dad. I wanted a unicorn to show up and say, "Hey your mind is a bitch. Your dad is fine, he just..." Blank. Who was I kidding? There was no good explanation for this whole thing. If he had early onset Alzheimer's and forgot where he was going, that would be an issue. If he stayed missing, that would be an issue. There was nothing positive about being missing for over 24 hours. He had no friends, as sad as that was to say. He kept to himself, as he had really bad social anxiety like me. But, well... he'd never had a reason to interact with anyone outside of our family for over twenty years. Even during parent-teacher conferences, my mom would do all the talking, and my dad would sit silently or stay home.

The afternoon ticked by and there was still no answer. No updates, as my mind decided to eat itself away. I was officially in zombie mode and did not feel like talking to anyone. I forced myself to make calls and tried to be engaged. Everything felt like too much, the surrounding noise amplified. My heart raced and I felt light-headed. I constantly felt that everyone knew something was wrong with me. I was starting to feel like I was walking around naked with my emotions out in the open. I needed to move away from my desk. I made my way into the kitchen at work. I made tea, stared into the mug, and took a deep breath. No one was in the kitchen. I could just stand there and take a sip or two and try to relax. Just as I took the first sip of tea, a co-worker snuck up behind me and tapped me on the shoulder.

"Aimee, are you okay?" She said, looking up at me with genuine eyes.

"Oh, yeah I'm just tired," I said, attempting to make myself seem believable.

I noticed my coworker, clenching onto her silver cross necklace. "Aimee, just so you know. I'm a Cancer."

"Wait...what?" I said, trying to hide my surprise.

"I'm a Cancer and I am great at listening. Seriously it's all in the stars." She said, smiling as though she found a way to break down my wall.

I tried holding back my laughter, I had not expected this kind of conversation. "I'll keep that in mind, Miss Cancer. Thank you."

"Wait. Why did you laugh? I'm seriously a great listener." She went to reach for my shoulder again, but I moved slightly to the left to avoid her touch.

"I just was not expecting you to say that. I wasn't sure how to react, but thank you. No, I needed that. Thank you, I appreciate you reaching out." I smiled and made my way back to my desk. Looking back at the odd conversation, I had not expected how quickly it had gotten so random.

Later that evening, once I got home, I received a call that the police had found my dad. Well, they called my mom and my mom told me. I told her that as much as he worried both of us, we couldn't start screaming at him—we would never get answers that way. Vince and I made our way out there. Vince was worried about me driving, as I was shaking from all the overwhelming anxiety I had been trying to bottle up.

This is what my dad told us: the day my brother dropped him off at Walgreens, he decided to go a mile in a different direction and take a walk in the woods. He walked around and took a seat on a nearby bench. His phone was dying so he decided he was going to turn around. However, he ended up falling asleep on the bench. When he woke up, he did not know where he was. Instead of returning home, he just kept walking in the woods, further and further away from where he was originally going. At one point, he realized he was lost and made his way back to where he started. He admitted that there were parts that were missing from his memory.

As he was telling me this, I hugged him and cried. All I could have thought about was, what if someone mugged him? What if he fell somewhere and no one found him until days later? As he finished explaining what he remembered, I looked at him and said, "We are finding you a psychologist. I don't care what you say. I will kidnap you if I have to. I will take off an hour early. I will figure it out."

My dad had tears in his eyes. Wait...was he crying in front of me? Other than finding his tears on him as he fell asleep all those dark nights, I'd never seen him cry.

"I do not want to get you fired. You might lose your job," he said nervously.

"Dad, I want to do this. If my work doesn't let me, then I will figure it out. Mom is a nurse, and works 60+ hour weeks. They most likely won't let her leave early. I am taking you, I will help you choose a psychologist. That is my final answer. I don't want to lose you dad."

I looked at mom, not looking for her permission, but making sure she understood that this was finally going to happen if it was the last thing I did.

Looking back at my dad, I simply told him, "I want you to be there when I get married. I don't want you to be sad and feel like you can't talk to anyone. I need to see a counselor. When we find you a psychologist, I'll go ahead and search for one too. Deal?"

I wanted him to know that he wasn't going to be alone. I did not care if I had to take him myself, wait for an hour, and then take him home. I was going to make sure that he went with zero excuses.

The next day at work, I knocked on my boss' door. I hardly talked to him after being hired. He was playing

Account Manager, Site Manager, Recruiting Manager... wearing multiple hats. I hated confrontation, I hated not knowing what the other person would say.

Taking a deep breath, I asked if he was available to talk for a few minutes. He said absolutely and asked how I was doing.

"I have to tell you something and obviously this stays between us. My dad needs to seek help, like, mental help, right away. I do not want him to make any excuses. I need to make sure he gets to his appointments. Most likely it'll be once a week. I know I work from 7:30 am-4:30 pm. If we find him a psychologist that would take him in at 5pm or after—I am aiming for after—would there be a way I can work 7am-4pm on those days so I can pick him up and get him to his appointment? I know that's a lot." My voice cracked towards the end, as I tried hard to slow my speech down. When I get anxious, I tend to talk fast.

He revealed to me that he recently had to take a family member for a psych evaluation for depression. He was more than understanding.

The next day, I grabbed my dad's insurance information from my mom and emailed some psychologists. I could barely stand making phone calls at this point at my work. I was not about to do it in unknown territory. Email is an anxious person's best friend. We ended up finding a psychologist that took on my dad as a client for two full years. I took him every Wednesday to his appointment for the first six months.

My dad changed for the better. He told us how he felt, he told us when he was feeling anxious or when his mind was playing games. He was put on medication for anxiety and depression. The psychologist also thought my dad had cabin fever. So, when he went on a walk, he felt free. My dad had depression and anxiety for 20+ years undiagnosed. He hardly left the house for long periods of time. I am proud to say that I am so thrilled with all that my dad has accomplished. He engages in conversations more, and he generally seems more confident. If you ever read this dad, you are my mental health hero.

CHAPTER 17:
Seeking Therapy From A Wizard

I was never diagnosed with depression in high school. I am sure it did not help that I hid some truths from my first psychologist. I did not meet the requirements based on the DSM-IV. The DSM is the bible for mental health professionals. It's a guide outlining multiple disorders, including what qualifies each disorder and what suggests an individual may have a specific disorder. I never met the criteria for depression in the DSM, because the criteria included experiencing a depressed mood and/or loss of interest for at least 2 weeks. The longest I felt depressed always was about a week. Then there were times I felt depressed for a few days and then randomly felt hyper. This also did not fit into the criteria for bipolar disorder. It left me undiagnosed and my condition was swept under the rug. I went on through high school and college with my depression never going away. I was often told that I was just a sensitive child. There was no label for me, and none of the correlations at the time existed. That was the DSM's whole point, a guide of correlations and finding out where the patient fit in with the correlations.

In September 2017, I decided to take a distinct step in my life. When my dad went missing back in 2015 for over 24 hours. I had made a promise to him that I would seek help as well. I pushed it off, and I simply told him that I was managing fine with my meds. The hardest thing in life, at times, is admitting when you actually need help. I didn't feel like I needed help for a while. I lived with my boyfriend who I loved, I had a career, a car, enough money for food and bills. Seeking help was only for people who really needed it right? I was completely fine and okay. My depression moods were getting a lot worse though. I felt panic and irritation for any little change that happened. Whether it was with work, or simply things out of my control like traffic. I decided it was time to seek a wizard, well, a counselor. Maybe if I just met up with someone once or twice I could see that I really didn't need help, that I was completely fine and just overthinking again. I just needed to slap the beast on the wrist and pretend I had full reign and control over everything I was feeling.

The morning of the appointment was nerve-wracking—how do you even begin? Was it justifiable to start seeking one out now? I stood in my kitchen, my two cats looking at me, perhaps knowing that my self-doubts were creeping in. This whole thing was going to be pointless. I could keep going through life like this, I've done it before. Things did feel a lot worse just then, but I kept telling myself it was no big deal, that I could just suck it up as I always had. Then I looked down at my cat and started speaking out loud, as if he was my therapist.

"Hi, I'm Aimee, I've been feeling depressed, but I know it hasn't been for two weeks. Sometimes I get hyper modes where I can't seem to relax and want to get out, but my anxiety always stops me, so I suppose it's a safeguard against rushing out while manic. I am a complete mess, like everyone else."

My cat looked at me, and then licked his butthole. While I highly doubt my therapist would respond like that, it would be very impressive flexibility on her end. My cat thought this whole thing was no big deal. Maybe that's what I needed to tell myself too. But there was a reason why I felt like I was barely hanging on. Perhaps talking to someone who saw things in a different light would help. I started jotting down everything I wanted to talk about, including what it felt like when my depression mode hit and what it felt like being anxious around people. Maybe she would diagnose me with being allergic to people? That would be a great excuse to avoid them and tame my anxiety. Unfortunately, that was not going to happen. The thoughts were persistent.

You are just wasting everyone's time.

Nothing is wrong with you... well, besides existing.

How pathetic are you that you think something is wrong with you? Everyone has it worse than you. You are just sensitive and stupid.

I placed the note in my purse and headed out the door. My appointment was only a few minutes away from work. Clenching the steering wheel, I thought about driving right past my psychologist's building. I could just tell her I forgot and try again another time. Instead, I followed the GPS to the parking lot. At that first appointment, I practically threw the note on the table and sat as far away from her as possible, constantly looking at the door.

Was it socially acceptable to run out and pretend I had a llama in the car? No, that would point out that I was irresponsible. Plus, who could forget a llama in the car? Crap! What did she just ask me?

I looked down at the floor, searching for a way to escape this situation. I took a deep breath and asked her to repeat the question. She asked about my history in regards to seeking therapy, if I had done so before. I told her about the time throughout high school. The words came out suddenly, the truth about how I dealt with depression and tried to hide it even with my therapist. She asked me what I was searching for in my therapy sessions. I told her I would love a "How to delete" guide in regards to experiencing my anxiety. While she said there was not a simple delete button, one of the approaches she practiced was acknowledging emotions, and facing them. Her sessions were open range in terms of going through what I wanted to discuss, reviewing notes on any anxiety triggers—the setting, how I responded, etc.— and ultimately finding ways to handle my emotions. I left the office feeling both relieved and nervous. I agreed to see her once a week, and we discussed that she would like to go over things like meditation, breathing techniques and self-awareness. Basically, staying in the present moment even when my brain went into various distractions and "what if" modes.

After many appointments and discussions, along with tracking my multiple moods throughout the day, she eventually asked me if I wanted to look at the DSM. Her viewpoint was that the DSM could help to see if you matched up with specific disorders. She compared it to astrology and how some people say they 100% match with their sign and some couldn't care less, but many grasp an understanding of themselves.

To start, we looked into Bipolar One and Bipolar Two. One of the qualifications for Bipolar One is having experienced a major depressive episode for two or more weeks. I did not meet that requirement, or a few of the others, such as having a manic episode for two or more weeks. However, next on the page was Cyclothymia. Cyclothymia is a disorder similar to bipolar disorder in terms of up and down emotions. However, unlike bipolar, it is "milder" and chronic. Suffering from Cyclothymia means you have experienced highs and lows that are persistent for two years or more. Everyone has their ups and downs—to be a disorder it has to affect your emotions and interfere with your daily life.

When the depressive episode hits (Armadillo Mode) the following can happen:

· Feelings of deep sadness, emptiness and hopelessness

· Irritability

· Feeling tearful

· Sleep disturbances—sleeping much more or much less than usual

· Social withdrawal

· Difficulty handling conflict

· Lacking meaning and purpose in life

And so much more...

During the hyperactive times, the following can happen:

· Inflated self-esteem, optimism—pretty much feeling like you are a badass motherfucker that can run with the lions.

· Racing thoughts and lack of concentration

· Talking faster and more than "normal"

· Easily distracted (probably doesn't help that I have adult ADHD too)

· Reckless thrill seeking—wanting to go by yourself or with a group of people to an unknown area and plot taking over the world with no money for instance. But maybe a random unicorn will appear and say hello—who knows.

And so much more...

Cyclothymia is its own category. Some sufferers even experience rapid cycling. Rapid cycling is exactly what it sounds like: constantly cycling through emotions, not only daily, but sometimes even in the same hour. Sometimes I experience these emotions for days at a time, and sometimes only for a few hours. There have been times where I've felt the urge to drive off, skip work and not care about the consequences—but then I realize I'd rather not live on the edge and get lost in something new and unknown. Then there are times, on those same days, where I feel at a loss, where I feel so incredibly broken that even a dog can't help me smile, where I can't even find a light in a bright summer day. On top of that, I have no real control over the transitions between emotions—sometimes they're just there for no reason and sometimes there are obvious triggers, like messing up at work, feeling like I said something stupid, alcohol, etc. This is another reason why telling someone not to be depressed is like telling someone to stop being cold when they are the ones in a tub full of ice and you're over there at the beach with perfect weather.

No two days are alike when it comes to Cyclothymia. Emotions change so quickly that not only does it confuse the outside world, it also confuses me.

Sometimes I will wake up and feel incredibly empty and useless as if I am not contributing to society and am just simply invisible. I'll go into work and focus on simply breathing and making sure I don't break for no reason. Sometimes I will feel like a curled up armadillo all day, or perhaps I'll switch to feeling up to my "normal self." But there are times when Armadillo Mode is so uncontrollable that I can't concentrate and my hyper side comes out, ready to fuck up my day further. This is often why I don't like to make 100% plans. If I am going to make plans, I want to be sure that I can back out of them safely if my emotional cycle requires—or simply if I am exhausted from fighting with myself and trying to seem normal. This alone has caused strains in my friendships, socials (or attempt of), side work, etc. I have to simply take each day bit by bit and learn my limits and just be okay with it.

On top of this, I also have General & Social Anxiety (Surprise!). Go big or go home, right? This is more than just having stage fright—which in my head is more than understandable to have. All those eyes and people staring at you... no thanks! With this disorder, social interactions are filled with irrational anxiety and you become a fear-wrapped ball of self-consciousness and embarrassment. What may not seem like a big deal for some is a big deal for me, like being called out to answer a simple question—anything from work or directions to food options can be a painful, heart racing experience. Some days are better than others, but there are times that I go to my favorite brewery and suddenly realize there are too many people to handle. My heart races, and I quickly look for an exit. I try my best to tell myself that all is safe. But if everything is still too much, I end up leaving early and looking to escape somewhere where there are no people. Which is also why, when I experience my hyper highs, I try not to act on them in a social sense. When I'm hyper I feel like I can take over the world and socialize...then I get to the event and either still feel hyper or end up having a panic attack and rush out.

Although I have many issues that are now defined in the DSM, (finally an answer!) I am not my disorder. Regardless of your beasts and/or your diagnosis, you are not that, by definition. A forest is a habitat for many creatures and plants. If a forest is filled with bunnies, the forest does not become a bunny itself. No matter what a forest holds, it still has many roots of history, cuteness, as well as the things that crawl in the dark. You are not a bunny, spider nor anything specific in the forest. The forest is the land of your mind. With beasts within, with people that may come and go. You are not your diagnosis but rather a forest that so happens to be a habitat for a beast that you may or may not carry. If that happens to be social anxiety, depression, bipolar or other types of beasts, try to remember: you are not the only land in the world that has this type of beast. Some beasts come in heavy armor, ready to fight. As they strategize to place those seeds of negative thoughts, feeding onto those negative emotions, waiting for you to give up and throw in the towel, it's hard not to compare our beasts to the beasts of those around us. But each beast is legitimate, with their own special abilities and weaknesses against certain medications, self-help, therapy and more. Every individual has the right to their own emotions. Even if it may not make sense, like, how can someone be scared of people? As quoted by my love, "You don't have to understand to help." There are plenty of people that are struggling with abuse, mental struggles, disorders and more. Just being there to help is one of the most important things you can do for someone in Armadillo Mode. You may not understand our flaming six legged beasts, but simply being there, hearing us out, and giving us ice cream (unless we are lactose intolerant, then prepare for some stink), are some of the most important and loving ways to help.

Pills, self-help, therapy and support from friends and family don't get rid of the beast. The help that we gain from ourselves and others are merely shields and swords, bug zappers for those anxious butterflies nipping at your skin. Each one of us has a skeleton that leans on us for support, even if it was part of a past life. Many have monsters, and no...pills don't make the monster(s) go away.

Medication and help are a form of protection, to see what is around us, and try to view things a bit clearer. We still feel the reactions from being hot. The thirst of dehydration, the sweat pouring down our skin—we are and can still be understandably hot. Forms of therapy, pills and so forth help. But it is by no means a magical route filled with happy singing animals or flowers. Nor would the random animals or flowers be singing "Hakuna Matata." Or maybe you do see that and have powerful drugs. I would not advise that though. Singing flowers would be creepy to say the least.

The light can still damage the skin, just as the darkness can sink its claws in. It's no wonder that when someone says, "I thought you were taking your pills," those dealing with their monster can react strongly. Some clench, feel horrible, and possibly even hold back some tears of anger. The pills help when we find that right formation that the darkness is weak against. If the monster is a fire type, you can't necessarily throw grass at it and expect it to be damaged. I mean, I guess you could...but it wouldn't be a logical thought nor action. Sometimes the monsters, including the demonic anxious butterflies, are singing "can't touch this," and we are in our eternal battle once more. We may damage a few for the time being and be able to breathe for a bit...but they are always wake up again.

Sometimes the beasts bring friends to help to plaster thoughts into our heads and keep us away from our own friends. Sometimes, the voices will say, "Your friends just feel like you have no one to fight for you. How pathetic." Or, "They feel pity for your soul. You have no right to live." The cries, the screams, aren't always displayed for all to see, but covered by multiple masks, backed up with different types of laughter, dark humor, etc. Just to get by. All I can say is this... it takes many tries to find out if you're better at defense or offense. Sometimes the challenges change as well, and a leader boss shows up to continue the beating. It's a whole point system of possibilities. Some days are better than others, where we can actually feel happiness and dance to the lights around us. Other times, the lights are around, but the feeling to dance is not. The urge to curl up in a ball, to become irritated and/or upset for no reason grows, and suddenly we feel distant from our own sense of self.

Trauma doesn't come with an expiration date. There's no set amount of time, tactics, or spells that will forever close the memories and the feelings. No medicine can cure the feelings forever. Medication is used to add additional armor to the monsters and beasts within. The combinations of therapy and having a great support system aids in fighting back. One of the parts of anxiety is the fact our brains see something as a threat. Even when it may not be an actual threat. The nervousness of walking into a room with people you may not know for an example, can wire our brains into thinking that a social situation is a threat. Years are not a definition of recovery. But how we handle and recognize our fears for what they are is part of the recovery process. Thus, our core beast lives on and should be recognized instead of ignored. Grab a cup of tea and handle the "I understand you are scared of this situation. What can we do to get through this?" Taking deep breaths, and acknowledging that there are going to be bad days and there are going to be good days. The bad days do not define that progress that you have made thus far. Just a reminder to take a step back and keep pushing forward in this odd thing called life.

"It is very hard to explain to people who have never known serious depression or anxiety the sheer continuous intensity of it. There is no off switch."

Matt Haig

CHAPTER 18:
Recruiting Mental Health

"Aimee, there are recruiters here that have been here for a year that are more confident than you are." I sat there, taking in my manager's words. Right...at this point. I had been recruiting for almost three years. My numbers on payroll and such did not match someone who had been with the staffing company for three years. Our plans and goals changed consistently to meet the demands of a fast-growing company. While he noted that I am one of the hardest workers there, I was also not where I should be, three years with a company and seeing some changes, including a new office, new staffing goals, and demands.

We recruit all across the country, mainly hiring traveling engineers, mechanics, technicians, laborers, and so forth. He had been my manager for two years at this point. The original manager who hired me moved out to Washington to open up our second office. My coworker and my mental health friend moved out to Washington to help open up the office.

I still made a few friends at the office, through odd circumstances and the newfound love of beer. However, I am, unfortunately, a person who takes a bit of time for change to sink in. I try to be as fluid as possible, go with the flow, and take life as it comes.

We expanded our staff almost three times over the past few years, which meant more people in the office, more demands for a fast-growing company. I sat there twiddling my thumbs, unsure what to say. It did not help that my anxiety-ridden brain, even on medication, was in a constant battle with comparing myself and overthinking. Perhaps that was my biggest downfall in the recruiting world at this point. I let people walk all over me and judged myself heavily. I remember emailing my manager that afternoon and told him, "I will do better; I was simply nervous about our phone roleplay," and left it at that.

Phone roleplays were the absolute worst thing in the world. The manager or another person acts like someone who is looking for a job. Sell them on the job, location, pay, go over their experiences, etc., then get heavily judged on what to do next. It's even more stressful because someone you know that is higher up than you is critiquing every little thing you do.

I have gotten a lot better over the years with my confidence in regards to talking on the phone. I still cannot order a pizza to save my awkward soul. I kept holding onto the idea that I am helping people find work. Every day I had to tell myself that I was not in a sales job, even though many times it felt like it was. However, I was an advisor of sorts with a dictionary of jobs available to candidates all over the country.

On the day of the roleplay, I was already having an anxious day. I stuck my neck out for a gentleman because he was late for his first day of work due to some car issues. He upped and left the next day because he did not like a particular worker at the facility. I felt a complete loss of control, and issues like this come up sometimes when you depend on someone else's commitment to a job.

After work in my notebook regarding my terrible anxiety day, I made some notes and set my tracker for my emotions I felt throughout the day. Bits of depression, thanks to my Cyclothymia and then full-on anxiety mode towards the end of the day. Luckily, I have been seeing my counselor for seven months, and our next appointment was tomorrow. I came home and felt shut down and exhausted once more; my brain is seriously my own worst enemy.

After going to sleep early and sleeping for over ten hours, I still felt tired and unmotivated to go to my counselor, let alone to my job. I felt a complete failure. Making my way into the same now-familiar building, I sat on the couch with my counselor as she asked me how I had been doing. I vented about work for perhaps a good thirty minutes. Going through my cycling of emotions, tiring myself out, anxious about how everyone else felt about me. I finally ended my rant with, "I am sick of trying so hard at something and not being good at it." She then asked me to clarify, "When you say you are not hitting your goals, are you saying your own goals or your company's goals?" I paused at her question, debating with myself and how to word what I wanted to say. "Shouldn't they be the same?

Shouldn't I find my success in a company's standards?"

She explained her thoughts on the fact of my overthinking and comparing myself to others. She mentioned that everyone had their starting points. Perhaps the recruiters that my boss had mentioned previously had been recruiters or worked at a call center previously. There was no way of really knowing unless I wanted to speak with my coworkers out of curiosity about their previous jobs. I thought about what she had said, reflecting on it. "So, I might set my own goals. I am doing my best, and I should keep in mind that I have come a long way from where I was at."

She nodded her head in confirmation, then added the following, "You are in control of the conversation between the person on the other end. I think that this is where you sometimes get anxious. When do you feel you are losing the individual, or they want to steer you? You are presenting them with your gift, as in yourself. There is only one you, with all your quirkiness, as you like to say. From our many conversations, you care a lot about people. Even when you feel anxious around them. You want to do your best and provide your services to helping people find work. Maybe in between calling people, take a deep breath, and remind yourself of that. Remind yourself that you are doing your best self."

The thought of my manager came into mind, as he would always say his famous quote of "Control what you can control." Perhaps that pertained to life as well. Although I still battle Anxiety and my Cyclothymia, I need to acknowledge that yes, I have come along way. Yes, I am not like everyone else, and that is okay. Every individual comes with their experience points and how they handle day-to-day life. I needed to focus on myself and set my own goals. I knew I was a hard worker; I just needed to control the person's conversation on the other line. Get to know them and their goals and focus on a career path rather than worrying about the sales end goal. This was something that I needed to focus on for my sanity. Attempt to try not to compare myself to other people. They may not have the same struggles or starting points that I had. That was my biggest take away from that day. To work on myself and find a system that works for me as I continue to go through my recruiting career. Perhaps in the future, I will explore other careers and avenues. For now, I needed to control what I could control. While sometimes people let me down, it was not a reflection of me and my self-worth.

I needed to focus on my message and find the right people for our clients. Have a plan set up and ready to go when I spoke with people. I also trusted my gut when they rushed me off the phone and said "Yes" to everything to try to rush me off the phone. This recruiting job allowed me to grow as a person and better communicate with people over the phone. I only have myself to compare to, and no one else. Plus, I could use this time to better myself and figure out what I may want to do in a few careers-wise years. Who says you have to stay at a job for 10+ yrs? As human beings, our goals change our passions throughout this life. As of right now, though, my goal was to become a part-time or full-time writer. The time will come, as long as I push towards my own purpose.

CHAPTER 19:
A Trip To Remember

"Aimee, you are going to Jamaica? Your poor skin!" one of my coworkers exclaimed. I was going to Jamaica at the beginning of 2018. I had never traveled outside of the country before. The closest I had ever gotten was Epcot at Disney World. For those who have never been to Epcot, various parts of the world are showcased at this Disney theme park, including Japan, Mexico, China, Norway, and more. That had been the closest I'd got. My parents would take us when I was young, perhaps before any of us realized that I was one anxious kid.

The trip to Jamaica would be with Vince's mom, Vince's little sister, and us. Vince's stepdad and little brother were going to stay behind because his little brother wanted to compete in the finals for baseball in his high school. I was still seeing my therapist at the time. We made cards that I could keep in my pocket, if I needed reminding to breathe and activities to calm my nerves. Just little reminders in my pocket so I wouldn't have a panic attack on the flight...or well...on the trip in general. February 2018 arrived quickly. At this point, Vince and I had already been dating for about seven years.

We had wine right before we boarded our plane to Jamaica. I had books ready to read throughout the long flight. It wasn't a terrible flight. From Illinois to Jamaica was about 4 hours. I assumed it was going to be a lot longer, but then again, I'm horrible with geography and directions in general. We landed in Montego Bay in the early afternoon and jumped on a bus to head to our resort. The bus ride was fine, other than being stuck with college kids that ruined the experience. Yes, I called them young college kids even though they were around 22 years old and I was 28 at the time; call me an old soul with less patience for most people each day. This guy that sat directly behind me kept saying snotty comments like, "Oh, yes, when my parents booked this trip this is exactly what I wanted to do, sit on a bus. I love this bus so much. What a great way to spend $600+ for a damn ticket. I hate them, I can't believe they did something so stupid." I looked at Vince, knowing he heard the conversation. He held my hand and just told me to ignore them. Well, yeah what else was I going to do? He never had to worry about me beating someone up or speaking up about their attitude. One of my anxieties included confrontation. So no bar fights ever for this one. Instead I just sat there, looking out the window and taking everything in.

We went to a place called "The Moon Palace" in Ocho Rios, Jamaica. It was an all-inclusive, family-friendly resort. I remembered to pack my medication, but I was worried that my depression or anxiety would show up on vacation even with the medication. On the first day while walking around the resort, I noticed there were a few cats that would wander around the site. No one paid any attention to them. Me, well I wanted to pet them. I made it my absolute mission to take a picture of each of the cats. Vince had to remind me that I probably shouldn't pet any of the cats; we didn't know if they were sick or anything. I simply told him, "Why would I do something so silly like that?" He knew... there was going to be a point that I was going to feel hyper and anxious, the cat would come on by, and I would want to pet the cat. Because, why not?

The funny thing with emotions and having mental disorders are the times they strike. Even though I was in one of the most beautiful places ever, my moods cycled through hyper/not thinking and anxious/depressed. I took my meds on time and monitored my drinking closely, but by the third day we told Vince's mom and sister that we needed a day to read in our room. They invited us to go downstairs to the pool; I'm sure Vince just told them that we were tired or had a migraine. Truth was, my Armadillo Mode had sunk in and I was worried about randomly crying at a restaurant or at the beach. I mean I suppose I could have taken a book and just made an excuse about a sad part in the book. But, well, it felt way deeper than that. I felt so overwhelmed and numb, and I just wanted to forget the world for a day. The monsters came with me to say hello and make sure I was aware that they were still there with me. I was in this beautiful place, and they still came. Which made me feel that much worse.

n the fourth day, I was tired, but I felt better compared to the day before. This time though, I felt hyper, anxious and ready to take over the world. It even got to the point of me picking up one of the outdoor cats while we were at an outdoor restaurant. As the salad was coming to the table, a cat walked past, just close enough to be petted and adored. Not really the most acceptable moment to claim "Kitty needs pets!" while being served salad and being reminded that... hey, outdoor cats most likely have fleas and such. But the cat didn't seem to mind it too much. It just became one of my many socially-not-acceptable and what-the-fuck-are-you-doing moments.

The next day, however, became one of the best and most memorable days of my awkward life. During our first few days in Jamaica I noticed there was a Gazebo on the far side of the beach. There was a wedding taking place and I fell into awe and amazement. I couldn't tell you how or why, but I always loved gazebos. My dream home would be a small ranch house or a cabin, with a gazebo out back for reading or perhaps some writing. When we arrived in Jamaica, Vince's mom had mentioned that she had a whole day planned out for Vince and I and that we would most likely be eating dinner on the beach. She also had a few other plans that she booked for us while she and Vince's little sister had a girl's day.

The plans involved a couple's massage, followed by swimming, a lunch date, and finally, the dinner date. As Vince and I made our way towards the beach, he took my hand and we headed in a different direction. Just as I was about to ask him where we were going, we came closer to the gazebo. There was a table, candles, and, most importantly, the gazebo was far away from everyone else.

"Whoever is eating there is so lucky. We should probably go before they come." I looked up at him, not thinking that perhaps the gazebo was for us. I thought perhaps he wanted to take a quick look because he knew how much I loved gazebos.

It was for us. Vince's mom had rearranged the couple's dinner so we could be in the gazebo. We had an amazing three course meal. I learned how to eat a lobster for the first time. When the lobster came and the waiter walked away, I started poking the lobster with my fork. "How is this to be eaten?" I asked. After my odd moment with the lobster, ultimately discovering one of my favorite foods in the world, dessert finally came on a decorated plate, a chocolate ball dessert on the side with the main dessert being cheesecake. I looked down at amazement, unsure where to start. Vince suggested that I start with the chocolate ball dessert.

Just as my fork hit into the chocolate ball. I heard a clunk noise as though I just hit something. A ring plopped out of the chocolate ball and rolled to the other side of my plate. I stared at the ring, stared back at Vince as he got down on one knee. This wasn't happening, no way. This...I was dreaming, that was it.

Well if I was dreaming, I would probably have a llama randomly show up. Nope, no llama, so...

I looked at Vince, as he was about to speak. "Aimee, I know it took a..."

A while? I did not care, as long as I was with Vince, I was happy with where I was at in life. We both wanted our own place, we both wanted to pay down some bills before we even thought of getting married. I thought of nothing other than...

"YES!" I yelled out.

I kept saying yes, tackling him as he was still on one knee, and making him fall to the ground. Yes, I tackled my now fiancé onto the ground. Vince's mom and his little sister came out of the bushes, laughing and recording the whole thing. So my tackling of my 250-pound fiancé was going to forever be saved. We made our way back to the hotel room, and I couldn't help but think how crazy he was. He had seen me at my worst, my emotional rollercoasters, randomness, and sometimes not having common sense regarding human interaction.

We got into bed, and I kept questioning him and making sure he was sure.

He laughed and held me tighter. "Yes, love. I am sure you are the one I want to marry."

I held him tighter, as I started kicking the sheets in pure excitement, overjoyed. Just as I looked at him, my foot made direct contact with one of his toes- and it made a solid crack noise. My eyes widened. Vince was surprised about the pain as he was half asleep.

Did I just break my fiancé's toe? Great, that was going to be an awesome conversation with his mom.

"Hey! Now that you are going to be my mother-in-law, you should know I am clumsy, and I just hurt your son in bed. No, not that kind of hurt. But more of the uh... I broke his toe." We ended up putting an icepack on it and he was able to move it after a few minutes.

He still wanted to marry this goofball that wants to have a goat, an emu, dogs and cats living with them. He knew once we got a bigger place, I was going to rescue a few dogs, or cats depending on what we already had at home. Indy and Sylvester would want to murder me if I ended up bringing another cat home. No doubt they wanted to be the only two cats in my life.

The next day, as a newly engaged couple, we went downstairs and treated ourselves to a peanut butter alcoholic drink. I definitely needed to explore the gym after this one-week vacation. I wanted to ask if he was sure once more. Perhaps he slept on it after I almost broke his toe. He got up to grab some breakfast, and his mom pulled me to the side. She hugged me and asked me how I was feeling. She was so excited; she had become my second mom even before we got engaged. She was one of the most hard-working, badass women I had ever known.

"You know, when Vince first met you, he came home and tossed his backpack on the couch. I was doing dishes and he told me that he met the girl he was going to marry."

Before I could say anything, she continued.

"I told him that was great. Who was she? He told me all about you and said you were dating some guy named Owen. You took my son's heart the first moment he met you. He told me that you just didn't know what you deserved."

I smiled at her; Vince and I had been friends for about a year give-or-take before I broke up with Owen and everything naturally fell into place. I remember hugging her and thanking her for always being my second family. Vince came back with a few breakfast treats for me.

After eating breakfast and making our way to the airport, I nudged Vince on the bus.

"You know you are crazy for marrying me, right? Like... I'm crazy, I'm weird, I'm awkward and..."

He kissed me on the cheek and placed his hand on the side of my face.

"I promise, I've been sure for years. Besides, you're my type of crazy."

I placed my head onto his shoulder, slipping into sleep and dreaming of all the things we would do in this life together.

Learning To Love Again Poem

Imagine all that you could achieve,

If self-love was accepted.

The feeling of righteousness to one's emotions.

Becoming more than a mental wish,

on a shooting star.

Continuing on life's path of multiple seasons,

Accepting the opposites of our mental state.

Day by day taking one breathe at a time

Knowing over and over again you are loved

And have a right to live.

CHAPTER 20:
Kai Addition of 2018

Vince and I had had several conversations at this point in regards to adopting a dog. I knew for a fact I wanted a dog that had already lived with cats in the past. Vince and I agreed that it was perhaps best to wait until after we got married on October 13th, 2019. After our wedding day and our cruise honeymoon, we talked about getting a smaller dog for our first dog together.

However, life has other plans. A year before the wedding, October 2018, on my way home from work one day, I spotted a new Animal Care Center. This route was the same route I had taken every day for the past few years. The Animal Care Center opened up perhaps a few months before I spotted it. I drove past it as usual, and then I started thinking about Indy and Sylvester. I had meant to find a vet for them that was a bit closer to home. This would be a great opportunity to check this place out. I kept telling myself, I could do it—in and out. I thought I'd go in there with a goal in mind, knowing what I was doing. I'd ask about plans for senior cats, and then leave and not make any crazy decisions until I got home thought about it. I am sure my cats would be hissing at me right now for even mentioning that they are now in the senior category of life.

I turned my car around and parked at the facility. There were only a few other cars. Assuming three out of the eight were staff members, it did not look overly busy. I took a few minutes to breathe and be aware of my surroundings, focusing on the present rather than the tricks my mind was trying to play on me. I told myself nothing would happen, I would be in and out in a few minutes. I walked into the bright and beautiful building, straight to the desk. I grabbed a brochure and started looking at it. When the receptionist got off the phone, I asked about the center's plans in regards to X-rays, as I knew one of my cats might need an extraction. They had affordable prices, senior cat plans, deals, and I could bring them in as often as I wanted on the plans for no charge.

Mission accomplished! I should have gotten myself a tub of ice cream on the way home for not having a panic attack. I was nervous, yes but I felt in control. Just as I was leaving, I saw a few kitties that were up for adoption. I decided to walk over to them. One of the cats had black, brown and a bit of cream coloring. I looked at the kitten and I could hear my cats sharpening their claws in preparation for revenge in my sleep. They were my babies, even if they were senior cats. They would make sure I no longer slept if I brought home another.

A lady came out from behind a door near the display of kittens wearing a shirt that said "Adoption Staff" with the logo for the shelter she worked with.

The lady smiled and asked "Hello, do you need help? Are you looking into adopting?"

Quickly, I responded with "Oh no, thank you."

Just as the lady turned around, I said "Well, not yet anyway. My fiancé and I talked about adopting a dog, but not until after we get married. You don't happen to have any dogs that have lived with cats before do you? I mean there are a few specific things we want in a dog."

My eyes looked down at the ground, nervous about how I must have sounded. Lack of confidence perhaps? Nervous at basic human interaction? Both were true.

The lady turned to look at me, as though anticipating I wanted to say more.

"We have two very active male cats. They are senior cats but they are completely crazy. They will run up and down the stairs, tackle each other, walk in front of anyone. So, when we adopt a dog, I want one that has lived with a bunch of dicks. I mean cats!" My eyes darted at the door. I could make up an excuse and leave, never to return.

The lady smiled, went to the reception desk, and pulled out a packet of dog listings.

"Does age matter to you?" She asked.

"We would like a dog at least a year old. No younger, preferably." I said grasping at my newfound confidence. I was absolutely sure that I did not want to adopt a puppy.

The lady smiled, "We have two dogs that meet your criteria. The first dog we have is Kai. She came to us back in August 2018, very much pregnant and very sick. She had her puppies a week after she came to our shelter. Now, I know for a fact she was fostered with cats from August 2018 to about a week ago when she got spayed and became ready to be adopted. The second dog, also female, is around 3 or 4 years old. Very healthy, we were told she came from a household of cats, but the family fell on hard times and had to give up their dog for adoption. Do you want to meet them?"

With little thought or hesitation, I quickly blurted out "Yes!" Without looking at the pictures, I met Kai first. The lady took me to the back of one of the exam rooms and I waited just a few minutes before meeting Miss Kai. The lady left us alone and gave us a few toys to play with. As soon as I met Kai, I forgot what Vince and I had talked about—waiting until after we got married. I played with Kai; she was estimated to be a little over a year old. She was tan with mixes of white and black throughout her coat. Her one eye was a beautiful ice blue, while the other one was half ice blue and half brown. She was a lean dog, a bit underweight, even considering the fact she just had a few puppies two months prior. I took out my phone and started videotaping her. I sent the video to Vince while he was at work.

According to the video, I kept saying "I cannot wait to bring you home and train you."

The lady came back a few minutes later and took Kai away. She asked me if I wanted to meet the second dog. Something felt right with Kai. I asked her right away for the adoption papers and told her that I would need to talk to my fiancé when he got home. I asked her if we could come back the next day after work so Vince could meet her too. She said Kai had someone else come in earlier today that might be adopting her. My heart sank, and I nodded my head telling her I understood.

After coming home that night, Vince was a bit surprised I didn't just grab Kai and come home with her. I was surprised myself, but at the same time I knew how important it was that he was in on the last-minute decision. I already had her picture saved on my phone, even though I kept telling myself not to set my heart on this dog. By the time we got there someone else could have already adopted her. Or she would not like Vince and then we would have to discuss training and to take the time to get her used to him. In my heart, I knew Vince would not have a problem with that. He knew for a fact that I wanted to save dogs in the future that were hard to adopt. We met at the Animal Care Center. I grabbed vet records for Indy and Sylvester, a letter from our association (even though we owned our condo), and three letters of reference. I wanted to do everything possible to get that dog.

After our initial interview, Kai went straight to Vince and cuddled him. She knew. She knew she already won my heart and had to win the heart of Vince. I could have jumped up and down in excitement, but I also did not want to scare Kai by suddenly transforming into a little kid. We went to the store and spent money on a kennel, dog food, leash, collar, calming treats, stomach ache treats, etc. We knew what we were getting ourselves into, and felt more than ready to take her on.

Indy and Sylvester were standing at the top of the stairs, looking down at us. As if we had come home late and they were the parents. Kai wagged her tail in excitement at seeing the cats. We did slow introductions. Kai wanted to groom them...licking them and wanting to cuddle with them. She actually would start whining when the cats paid no attention to her. Indy and Sylvester did not want to be groomed at all. The first week of adoption went great. We attempted to put her in her kennel at night. We were worried that she would get anxious during the night and chew on stuff. She barked, whined, and would have nothing to do with her kennel. By the fourth day we let her roam free and she ended up cuddling in bed with us. During the first week or two she greeted everyone. Every single person, every single leaf, every single blade of grass. After that, I think she got comfortable and knew she wanted to protect us.

Any1 time we have company over, we tell the guest to ignore Kai and let Kai come up to them if she wants to. New people mean slow movements, treats and encouragement. She was our medium size guard dog that wanted slow introductions. She was actually awkward with some dogs too. She's a very sensitive lady who has to sniff a dog's butt first before face-to-face interaction, unless she gets comfortable with a dog. So, if a puppy starts going right at her face, she nudges them away and tries to sniff their butt. Thank goodness people are not required to do such things.

It has been two years since we adopted Mamma Kai. That is her nickname at small doggy day camp. While she is a Husky-Cattle dog mix (We have no idea, the adoption and vet papers said two different things), she is most comfortable in small doggy day camp. The staff members said that Kai makes their job so much easier, even though they have to sometimes remind her that they can handle it. Kai will sit and watch the dogs and play, and the moment she sees them playing too roughly, she will walk over to them and separate the pups. Yep, she is a momma dog for sure.

I would be lying if I said I never avoided events or new locations because of my social anxiety. I would be lying if I said I was not at all nervous going to a new place. However, I will say this: I am so grateful that I went to the Animal Care Center when I did. I am so glad that I forced myself out of my box and that I listened to my intuition. Kai has taught me so much in regards to patience, accepting our awkward quirks, and being okay with who we are. Kai will have good days and bad days. Sometimes, she will not want to greet another dog on our walks, and she will keep walking. I will never force an interaction, I have gotten better at being her voice. Kids will run by and ask if they can pet Kai. Kai is fine with kids as long as they are slow, otherwise, she gets scared and wants to walk away. I simply tell the kids, "Only if she wants you to pet her. Have her sniff your hand first. If she is interested, she will get closer. If not, then maybe next time." I suppose that is the same thing with social anxiety. There are good days and bad days. Making a note on our emotions, like, "today I feel anxious for no reason," can in turn become, "I need to allow myself time and space to take in my environment," and that is okay. Handling social anxiety, depression, and more, requires time to recognize triggers and allow ourselves to breathe.

CHAPTER 21:
DEAR 2019

By the time I got to writing this part of the book, I had shut down for six months. I didn't look at the book, I didn't even edit it—I put it on a shelf for later. I could blame my thoughts for this one: self-doubt and feeling like a fake. Not a fake for what I am writing, no. The whole point of this book was to be raw, full of emotion, full of humor, and laugh at life's awkward side. I felt like a fake because I kept asking myself: "Why do I feel like I can be a writer?" I worried so much about my own self judgements. I let my anxiety monster win. How could I think my writing would be good enough for others to read and hopefully enjoy? I took a few months off to collect myself, and then 2019 happened. Six months turned into a year. There is a saying at nursing homes, when it comes to the Grim Reaper knocking on the door: "Everything comes in threes."

A lot happened in 2019, and I debated whether or not to even add it to the book. Both my grandmothers passed away, as did my friend/co-worker. My father called me one Sunday morning in February and said, "Aimee, are you working right now?" Something in his tone told me something was wrong.

"No, dad. I'm not working right now. I'm off on Saturdays and Sundays. What's wrong?" I said, trying not to sound worried.

"My mom, I mean, Grandma, is in the hospital. They are assessing her to see if she had a stroke. I'll let you know when I find out more information. I love you." I could tell he had been crying. As his voice cracked, he had been trying too hard to stay calm, perhaps for me. Before I could say anything, he hung up the phone.

I later texted my mom, to make sure she was home with him. They were already on their way down to see her at the hospital. My heart began to weigh heavy, as I looked up at my husband who was playing a video game and had not heard the conversation. I tapped his shoulder and he took one look at me and saw my pain and worry. I knew there was no way I could hold back the tears.

"Love, what's wrong?" he said, as he stood up and hugged me tightly.

"Grandma..." I began to mutter "The nice one." I said, unsure where to begin. "She may have had a stroke, love. She's 93 years old. I don't know how she is going to handle anything if... she's not able to walk or..."

Before I could finish, my husband hugged me and told me to take a deep breath. He reminded me that going down into the "What ifs" was not going to help. All we could do was wait on the phone call and then act. We'd take the time to go down there to the small town, no matter what.

An hour later my mother called to give me an update. She explained that my Aunt Mary came home to check on Grandma. That was when Aunt Mary called her to explain that Grandma was slurring her speech. My mom advised her to take Grandma to the hospital to be checked in and evaluated. As soon as mom received the phone call, she told her boss she had to leave early and picked up my dad to go to the hospital.

It was a waiting game, as the hours ticked by. It was later confirmed that my Grandma had a major stroke. After much assessment, it was revealed that she had lost the ability to swallow and chew her food. Tuesday, I was told, she tried sitting up on the bed on her own. My mother said you could see the pain and frustration in her eyes as she stared at her legs and nothing was registering. There was no movement of her legs.

I could easily describe my grandmother as being "stubbornly independent." She lived on her own with my uncle who had mental deficiencies. After my grandfather died, before I was born, she did everything on her own. She was such a stubborn woman that even though the doctors suggested her having a walker just in case, it always sat there next to the coffee table, wedged in and hardly ever used.

She was the grandmother that tried to teach me how to sew. She would make quilt blankets by hand and I told her I wanted to help her make some. I never learned how to sew, I had zero patience for it. But she never once looked at me any differently. She always told me I could do anything I wanted to do. The days that I would stay at her house, we would play Checkers or Chutes and Ladders, and she would read me a chapter or two of *Chicken Soup for the Cat Lover's Soul* when I was really young and had a hard time reading. She always believed that I just needed to find my niche, my interest. After reading, she would ask me how the story made me feel. Every morning, she would take out a bowl of Wheaties and personally cut up strawberries for me. She was the grandmother that understood that people stressed me out, perhaps before I even knew. We would enjoy each other's company, and she would never force an interaction with me and the neighborhood kids. I was accepted by her, and I always had a safe place in her loving arms.

After her stroke, my grandmother was placed in hospice. She was later transferred to a Hospice Hospital. There was no sense in forcing tubes down her throat. Tuesday was the day she was in hospice. And that day I went up to my boss to tell him that my grandmother was most likely going to pass away in a few days. I took off Thursday night, and drove down with my husband. Well, I should say my husband drove because let's be fair—an anxious driver isn't always the best. We made our way to the hospice facility and were greeted by amazing staff. There were about 15 people total in the room. The room was absolutely beautiful, with artwork, two couches, a rocking chair, and a dining table. We all circled around my grandmother's bed. Her eyes were closed, and her breathing was shallow. The time was near. It had only been a few days since her stroke and I could see so many differences. At this point, it had been a year since I last saw her.

With my grandmother living a few hours away from us, I had made plans to show up to her house in my wedding dress. She could not handle long car drives, and I knew she wanted to be a part of it. I had planned on showing her my vintage wedding dress with lace throughout and the perfect fit for me. I'm not even a dress person, but I fell in love with my wedding dress. Did I mention it was on sale for less than $300?

At the hospice we all shared stories of how she used to make homemade pasta, how she would make strawberry shortcakes and make sure we were all taken care of. Or the stories of simply passing the food at the dinner table and her giving us this glare of "I'm not dead yet. I can handle myself." She was the complete opposite of my other grandmother. The stories involved all the cats that would show up to her place. I swear, there was a cat meeting every week to decide which cat would show up at her door seeking shelter. At one point she had 13 indoor cats, along with a few outdoor cats that she would grab to treat them for ticks.

Friday morning came, and everyone left the room except for me and my husband. I felt my throat clench tighter. I needed to say my goodbyes, without anyone else there. I sat next to my grandmother, brushing her thin white hair. I told my husband to close his ears for a minute. Then I whispered to my grandmother and tried my best to describe the dress. I do not remember what I said, other than, "Sorry, you're going to hear me say over and over that my dress is white because I am horrible with dress descriptions." I kissed her forehead, and the tears followed. I told her that I loved her, that it was okay, that we would be checking up on my uncle. We would make sure he was taken care of. I told her that she was one of the many reasons that I smiled. I told her she showed me how to always be myself, even if I was scared of people.

Friday night, my husband and I went out to McDonalds for a quick meal, during which my Aunt gave me a call and told me "It's time." Quickly we rushed out, and I clenched my hot chocolate. I tried to keep balance and stay grounded. I took deep breaths; the last thing I wanted to do was to faint outside of her room before her passing. I walked into the room and felt the cold feeling all around. I honestly do not even remember passing my hot chocolate over to my cousin and grabbing onto her hand. I remember the song that played, with her last few breaths. "Come to Jesus" by Chris Rice.

February 15th 2019

Grandma: I hope you know you were one of the most independently stubborn people I ever met. No matter how much others wanted to help you, you always refused. One of the priests from the church you went to showed up—he had tears in his eyes. I'm sure you already knew that though, you were one of the first people that went to that church when you were young. No matter how many times you'd shown me before, you would always show me the same pictures, the same antique items, each time I would come visit. You always had the jewelry, the pictures, the clothes to show me, and I looked at them as if it was the first time. I'm sure you already knew this, perhaps you are in heaven in a library full of cats. Make sure the cats don't knock over your coffee mugs too much, okay? You were surrounded with love, and I am sure that will continue. I held your hand as you took your last breath. I'm glad I was there. Thank you for everything you have done in this beautiful world called Earth. Also, thanks for not being completely weirded out by my oddness and lack of people skills.

March 16th 2019

My grandma on my mom's side's health was declining. I was never close to her. Honestly, throughout childhood I was very scared of her. I would stay at nice grandma's house for a week and a half, then spend only a few days with my other grandmother. I could never make it the full three days with her. She always ended up dropping me off for being too much or too much of a hassle. She declined so quickly, within days. My grandmother passed away due to her dementia. There were times when my mother told me, "Wow, I think mom forgot she was mad at me," and went about her day. My grandma had to be transferred to a few different hospitals. She tried breaking through the window, bit a doctor's arm, and was scared. No matter how negative my grandmother was towards me, no one deserves that. No one deserves their whole world being turned upside down so that they can no longer recognize anything around them. She forgot her horse's name, and only then did her children realize how bad everything was getting.

I was prepared for both of these. I cried and was able to say my goodbyes one last time. Though, with my grandmother on my mom's side, I only got to say goodbye at the funeral. Everything came apart piece by piece...even to this day I still miss them. I am reminded of their flaws and love. The feeling of death, and what came towards that creeping moment of realization they were going to be gone; I would no longer be able to call and check on them. I wouldn't be able to wish them a happy birthday, nor receive a card in the mail with their signature. Life would be different, moving forward with these gentle reminders of how much of an impact they had on me, with them no longer being around and in it. Both of these deaths were hard, but I had time to prepare for the Grim Reaper.

August 17th 2019

As I am writing this, I am on the verge of tears. Thursday, August 15th my world changed once more. There is no right way to tell someone of the passing of a passing coworker, friend, or family member. My manager, the owner of the company, walked into the office and told everyone to get off the phone. As recruiters, we needed to always stay on the phones— this was different. I stood there in the circle as we surrounded the owner of the company. She was always sweet, kind and usually so positive and upbeat. I could tell she was on the verge of tears. I knew; I didn't want to know...but I knew. I could feel the color in my face drain away. A friend and coworker of mine moved up to Washington to assist with opening the new office. He and I stayed in touch and ended up becoming mental health buddies. We would check up on each other weekly. He had just gotten engaged to his girlfriend. He joked that I would approve of her, since she was a huge animal lover (I approve. I wish I met her, but I was so happy that you were finally happy).

I hadn't been able to reach him for a few days, but I knew he was busy with work. But then he didn't show up to the office all day. HR had been trying to get a hold of the police to do a wellness check. They had also been trying to get a hold of his family to see if they heard anything. Although it had been less than 8 hours, this wasn't like him. He was the kind of person that never showed up late, because tardiness would cause an anxiety attack. If anything, he would call into the office if he felt that he was going to be even a few minutes late.

Snapping back to the present, my boss spoke to everyone. The words began as a first of many: "There is no easy way to say this..." followed by the name of someone that meant so much to me. There is no magical unicorn that can be brought from under the ground perfectly ready to present the news. As if even that would lessen the blow.

If there were, the unicorn would stab its horn right into your heart, twisting it and making you feel pale, faint, causing a tunnel vision effect as the rest of the words that followed echoed. "There is no easy way to say this but your co-worker was found dead in his apartment. We don't know the details on how it happened. He was just recently engaged and had several conversations with people the night before. No signs of foul play or burglary were found."

I felt a hand touch my shoulder. Or, I should say, I knew the presence of that hand there. I have no idea who touched me at that moment; all I could focus on were the words screaming in my head. NO NO NO NO NO. THIS ISN'T REAL. I NEED TO WAKE UP. I FELL ASLEEP AT WORK. Something, anything, would be better than that moment. The unicorn twisted its horn once more, forcing me to confront the fact that this was the truth. I wanted to escape and yet felt so incredibly heavy. Once the meeting broke up, a few people went back to the phones to work. I went back to my desk, another hand went on my shoulder, and this time, I heard the words: "If you need a few minutes." I wanted so badly to say I needed a few more days. I needed to talk to him again, I needed and wanted to say how much I cared about him. I screamed in my car on the way home. I have never screamed or yelled in my car...not like that. I remember the sheer panic that I felt. My throat became raw as the tears would not stop flowing.

My fiancé was still at work, otherwise I would have asked him to pick up Kai from doggy day camp. I made my way to the familiar parking lot, parked the furthest away from the building. Checking the mirrors to make sure I did not look like a complete mess. All the points for not being someone who wore makeup. I made my way to the building, feeling numb and frozen to everything around me. The last thing I wanted to do was start randomly crying my eyes out in front of people. As I stepped into the building, I saw a corgi making its way to its owner. Fluffy self all smiling and greeting the world with its fluffy butt. I smirked a little at the excitement of the corgi. I wanted to ask to pet the corgi, in hopes of distracting myself once more. The words did not come out, probably for the best. One of the doggy day camp workers that I see regularly saw me and I think she knew something was wrong. She was normally bubbly, but she just simply said "I'll go ahead and grab Kai for you." Kai ran up to me, and was ready to leave the building. I placed her on the back seat of my red car, bucked her up tight and kissed her face.

"Kai, you may not know why. But today is a tough day. We need treats. Lots of treats."

We made our way home, as the cats meowed for attention. I would like to think they knew something was wrong. They were cuddly as normal, but they followed me around way more than normal. I gave Kai her doggy ice cream and placed some dog friendly peanut butter on it. As she was inhaling the ice cream and wagging her tail, I opened up a bottle of wine and started a hot bath. I let the tears fall, as I stared at the water filling up the tub. How was I even going to tell Vince? Vince never met my friend before. But he would take one look at me and know something was wrong. How could I even word such a thing "Hey, you know my one mental health buddy, yeah he's dead. So, I am having wine all night tonight." Vince soon came home from his twelve hour shift. He was recently promoted to site manager at another hospital. Things seemed to be going up, after my grandmother passed away early this year. He sat there with me on the floor, as I laid in my bath and just cried without hardly any of it being audible. Finally, the words came out and Vince left to make me a grilled cheese and ham sandwich. I knew I needed to eat, especially after finishing a whole bottle of wine. I slowly managed, in between the tears and finally getting out of the bathtub, to have my late night sandwich. How was I going to go to work tomorrow?

The next day, Vince asked me if I was going to call off. I told him no, and I would just need a distraction. One of the longest days ever, as my coworker went up to me and simply said "He was a great worker." Yes, I am clearly upset because we lost a great coworker. Not that I lost a friend, lost a person in my life...again. I somehow managed to barely hit my call goals and had little patience for small talk over the phone. Not that I had any patience for small talk to begin with.

A week passed and Vince and I ended up going to the wake. There were so many people there, but I did not care. My hands clutched onto Vince's. They ended up cremating my friend. I think that is what he would have wanted. There was a long line of people to talk with his parents and pay their respects. Throughout the long line there were posters of him as a kid, his favorite sports, and so many flowers. I only said a few words to his parents, I couldn't bare anymore. They probably had no idea who I was, but I doubt it mattered to them. A son gone too soon, no parent ever wants to go through that.

After we left, Vince and I went to the grocery store to grab a few snacks and perhaps some bubbles for a hot bath for the weekend. I made my way to the beanie babies that I saw near the face mask section of the store. Sitting there by itself, was a pink sparkling platypus that looked pissed off at the world. I grabbed the platypus and walked over to Vince and simply said "He looks pissed off. I'm getting this platypus. I'm already over this damn year." And sitting in the cart was the pink, pissed off platypus. Pissed off that it was pink? Pissed off that it had big 'ol eyes for all to see? Who knows. But all I cared about was the fact that I wanted to grab something for myself, and it seemed like it was my spirit animal at this point. Days became weeks and weeks became months.

As I am writing this, it has now been a little over a year since his departure from this world. I still get choked up—and honestly, that is okay. There is no time limit on feeling loss, nor is it true that "time heals everything." Because it doesn't. It takes time to adapt, that is true. However, there is not a blueprint that says, "Okay, after 6 months you'll never be reminded of the person again." I think one of the hardest things is giving ourselves self-love and understanding during the worst of times.

We tend to be our own worst critic when it comes to judgement and feeling the need to diminish ourselves for our responses. It's okay to hold on to the memories of those who have been lost. It's okay to still miss them, even years later. We already give ourselves enough of a hard time in this world. So if we feel an emotional tug or reminder of someone at random – at a grocery store, sitting alone, or eating dinner – it's okay to be alive and missing someone.

CHAPTER 22:
The End... For Now

I walked with my father down the aisle. I was consumed with both nervousness and excitement. My father was on the verge of tears the moment he saw me in my white dress. So much had happened in our relationship over these past few years. He decided to see a therapist after I thought I lost him forever. He still had his paranoid thoughts that stemmed from his depression. However, he was more vocal about it; he took more walks to ease his mind and talked with people which took so much weight off of his shoulders. I am so incredibly proud of my father and that will always bring tears to my eyes. Will there still be times when he calls me up, anxious about something coming in the mail from someone he doesn't know? Yes. Most often, it is spam. They do not have your life information and please do not give anyone your SSN by text or mail, especially an unknown company. Will there be times that my heart jumps when I see my mom or dad calling? Yes, because I always anticipate something wrong, but that has gotten better.

More importantly though, during the father and daughter dance, my dad began to cry and said, "I remember those days when you tried to find daughter-father events when you were in high school. I always told you no, and I am so sorry."

I hugged him tightly and assured him I did not remember any of that—which was the truth. I told him that all that mattered in that moment was that we were dancing together, that we were in the same room despite our social anxiety with the world. Despite the depression that life threw at us, we were there in the present and alive. My father had been so nervous about ruining my day by doing something wrong. That was his depression and self-doubt talking. I hugged him tightly and assured him if he stepped on my dress we would just laugh it off together. I was bound to fall or break a glass before the end of the day anyway.

We walked down slowly. I knew my father was incredibly nervous as well. But we were in it together. My fiancé's smiling face was waiting for me—I wanted to run over to him. I was so excited and nervous with the crowd that I just wanted to be in his arms. The ceremony itself was nice and short. I almost felt as though I was going to faint with all the eyes looking at us. However, knowing that I was up there with my future husband, and we were sharing this moment together, kept me upright. I quickly noticed a pin he was wearing. A pin that I selected from my grandmother's jewelry to have, to keep and wear. The golden angel was pinned perfectly to his navy blue suit jacket. The original plan was to have the pin on my dress, but with all the lace it may have ruined the fabric. The navy blue with the gold worked wonders though. Everyone asked him about the pin and its special meaning.

"This was a pin that Aimee's grandmother had and always wore. There has been a lot of loss this year. They are right here with us though."

After the dances came the speeches. Vince has always been one of those people who can just get up on stage in front of everyone and create the best speech ever with zero stresses. I on the other hand would probably start rambling about llamas and run off forgetting where I was going because my nerves would get the best of me. As the microphone went around, I nudged at Vince, asking what he wanted to do. I knew the time had come.

Vince's mom had been married three times. The first marriage was for a few years and Vince gained two sisters that he hardly talks to but will always consider his sisters. In the second marriage, Vince's little brother and little sister were born. He helped deliver them and cut the cord because the second husband wanted nothing to do with the gross stuff. Plus, during that time Vince's mom was a midwife and decided it would be best to deliver her two children at home. A few years passed and the second husband ended up leaving. The third husband, Pete, Vince would forever call his father. Pete came into Vince's life when Vince was already in high school. After experiencing the first two failed father figures, Vince was distant with him. However, from the very beginning, Vince saw that Pete was different. Pete took on the kids as his own. In the beginning of the relationship, Vince's mom broke her neck and Pete took it upon himself to cook, take the kids to school, pick them up from school, help them with their homework, all within a few months of them dating.

Vince stood in front of our 90 guests and began to speak. He thanked everyone for coming, for all their support and love. He stood by the cake that was decorated as a pile of books. He went through each book on the tier.

The first was *Dresden Files*, a series that he and I both enjoyed watching and reading together at the very beginning of our relationship.

The second was *The Obsidian Trilogy*, a series that got us talking about books and connected as more than just friends.

The third book was *Furiously Happy*, the second book by Jenny Lawson. He joked that the first book called *Let's Pretend This Never Happened* probably would have not been appropriate for part of a wedding cake. I mean, unless the ceremony was so bad that that everyone wanted to forget. He casually talked about how it spoke about the humor and awkwardness that life brings, all while talking about mental health.

Finally, there was *10 Stupid Things*. This book covers subjects of women and men falling prey to playing roles, like White Knight, that might not suit them. It pretty much covers dating all the wrong people and realizing you deserved better all along. Vince read the male version, I read the female one. *10 Stupid Things Men Do* and *10 Stupid Things Women Do*. Welcome to rescuing people that do not wish to be saved!

Towards the end of his speech, Vince looked at Pete and casually said, "My mom and I have been through the toughest of times. There were times that this woman went days without eating to make sure I was fed. She got into nutrition because I was a pain in the ass baby being allergic to everything under the sun."

Okay that part I am summarizing. Vince didn't swear in front of everyone on the reception floor.

He continued, "However, I would also like to talk about my dad Pete. Pete, if anyone here says you are not my blood, just ignore them. You are my blood. You have been with me way more than any other person who took my mother's hand and said, "I do." You are my father, and I want everyone to know that you are my dad."

Pete and Vince had a long memorable hug. Then, we continued our rounds thanking everyone for their love and support.

The wedding went perfectly, though I wish we had more time to eat our own food. Note to those getting married: allow yourself more than 30 minutes to eat your food. You will want to relax, have some wine, and you'll be walking around talking to everyone all day.

October 13th, 2019.

The year was hard and long, with many tears and heartbreak. I am forever grateful for those that have supported us along the way. A toast to new adventures and life of the socially awkward—be prepared my love, my family, my friends. Life is full of ups and downs, and emotional trials. The people in our lives help us make it through; them, and a sense of humor. We make it through awkwardness, in health and even when I accidently cut myself on the aluminum foil of a wine bottle. I will continue to exist and push through this odd thing called life. Just as many others continue to fight and be the amazing warriors they are today.

Odd Acknowledgements of Importance:

My Love:

Where do I even begin? Let's talk about Llamas and Alpacas first. Oh! Wait, we need to have our very own petting zoo... without the people. Goats, llamas, alpacas, lambs, and bats. I know, bats don't belong on farms—but hey, I can dream, right? No matter how random, and atypical I am, you love me for me. You wouldn't change a thing about me (well except for the fact I'm a bed hog—not my fault you're a warm furnace!). You are a complete smart ass. Sarcastic, understanding, emotional, kind and... did I mention a smart ass? You have always been supportive of me. Anytime I suggest a dream that is book-worthy, you always say, "And you haven't written it yet because?" Because I have self-doubt, but you have encouraged me to look past that and DO IT. You are my one and only love, absolutely my forever. I get to love you, and it is the best thing that I'll ever do.

My parents:

Oh, my parents! If you get a hold of this book, I'm sorry. I know, my brother and I grew up with the notion of keeping things to ourselves. I wanted to write this book because of the oddities of life, which included you guys. You guys are one of a kind. Despite the circumstances of your past, you loved my brother and I unconditionally. Were we stubborn teens? Yep! You bet. Did I use to get embarrassed by you telling the stories of my Beanie Babies history lesson back in Elementary School? Yep!

Disclaimer note: It wasn't the history of Beanie Babies. Instead, we would use the Beanie Babies to playout wars, presidents, and events in the past. I was embarrassed before, but now it's only cute and sweet.

You guys are amazing, and I wouldn't trade you for a world of unicorns and dragons. And that's saying something! Just know that I do get into some in-depth topics from childhood and college that you may or may not have known about. I love you guys. I am lucky to have you in my life.

To My Brother:

You know that stereotypical little sister that is annoying and follows their big brother around? Yeah, I overfilled that stereotype. To be fair, though, you threw Tigey on the Burger King roof. You swung him around by his tail and onto the roof he went. I had to get my revenge somehow. Tigey could have made Burger King his home if it wasn't for a worker getting a ladder to go on the roof for it.

I will always remember you defending me and winning the fights against bullies even if my memory is wrong. You have always been someone from which I wanted to get approval. Through high school and college, we grew apart. You ended up graduating high school early, all while avoiding people–I was kind of jealous that you were going to school at home. However, I am happy to say that we have rebuilt that relationship. If you are reading this book, be prepared for many untold truths and randomness. Surprise?

My friends:

My first of many drafts listed each person, and ended up being almost two pages long. I had to cut it a lot. My dear friends who have encouraged me, not only with this book but helped me to keep fighting. You guys are amazing. I wish that I could do so much more. I know I can tend to be motherly, in the sense of being protective and making sure you're okay. I know, at times, I have a completely different conversation in my head and then assume you were involved in it.

To my Editor:

Thank you for not burning my book with all the grammar issues. Please know that I was having extra wine on your behalf. Or perhaps you were already drinking some throughout. Thank you for all your support and all that you do. Also, writing is a learning process and I should have sent my book to my beta readers first and then to you. So you had to look at my book twice! The horror! If we ever meet in real life, remind me to buy you some wine.

To My Readers:

Wow! You're getting a book from someone you have no idea about. I could be the most annoying person out there, and here you are, not only reading my book— but you took a risk! Eek! I hope that I made one of you out there smile with my crazy life. You are an individual. Your very own history book of your past. Your past does not seal your fate. We have the right to our emotions but must take responsibility for our actions. If you bought this or borrowed it from a friend, I will say, thank you so much. I had my doubts about what the point was. But then I realized, if my experiences and odd ways can help someone at least smile, then why not?

Know if we ever meet, I am very awkward and may run away. I may be more approachable if you happen to have an animal with you. Then I will talk up a storm with just the animal's presence. So let's say this, if we ever meet in real life the requirements of association is to have an animal. Dog, cat, llama, alpaca, platypus, etc. Though, if you do decide to go the platypus route they are one of the few mammals that are venomous from their hind feet! Well, before I get distracted from writing on animals let me focus on you, the reader. Thank you so much for giving my book a try. As a first time author, there have been a few bumps and learning curves in regards to writing. I found that, after I was done with the first draft I put my book away for a while and went back to it with fresh eyes. I hope that my book, my story, has helped you in some way with navigating your way through this awkward thing we call life. I am planning on writing more, and perhaps my editor won't need so much wine as I get better with grammar and so forth. Be safe and peace be with you!

We are all warriors, even when Armadillo Mode takes over.

Made in the USA
Monee, IL
13 May 2021

68507462R00118